# YESTERDAY'S RAILWAYMAN

# YESTERDAY'S RAILWAYMAN

## D. A. Newbould

**Oxford Publishing Company**

Typesetting by:
Aquarius Typesetting Services, New Milton, Hants.

Printed in Great Britain by:
Hollen Street Press Ltd, Slough, Berks.

Published by:
Oxford Publishing Co.
Link House
West Street
POOLE, Dorset

# CONTENTS

# INTRODUCTION

I can remember, as a small boy in the late 1940s, standing on Mexborough Station in South Yorkshire watching all the trains going past, and writing in my engine book all the numbers of the different engines. But unlike most engine-spotters I was fascinated by the No. 2 signal box, which stood rather grand and proud just off platform 1.

I used to listen with awe to the sound of a strange system of bell ringing, levers moving and telephones while, at the same time, trying to work out what they all meant. These were my first memories of a working signal box.

With nearly all the old type of signal boxes, with the block telegraph system, now gone, I felt it would be a pity if such a vivid part of railway life were to disappear without recording the hard work, dedication, fun, and characters that were the signalmen, so I decided to write this book, this being a true story of my career spent on the railway.

I have not set out to go into technical details or to feature any particular railway and, although my story is set in the Eastern Region, it could easily apply to any other region. The incidents and all the characters are true, and are recorded as I remember them.

Although there is a magic about steam engines and engine drivers' tales, I hope this book will give another look into the lesser-known side of railway operations, by including not only signalling, but train control and clerical duties.

# Chapter One
# Schoolboy Ambitions

Mexborough, in South Yorkshire, is a small town surrounded by heavy industry, and is situated between Doncaster, Rotherham and Barnsley. Because of the industrial scene, it was a haven for schoolboys interested in railways.

The area is mainly freight orientated but, with a local passenger train service plus a few express passenger trains, there was a good selection of everything; not only different trains, but different railways, at one time totalling as many as twenty. Mexborough was at the heart of the Great Central Railway with GCR style buildings, signals, signal boxes and stations still very much in evidence. Near to my home there was the old London Midland & Scottish Railway and eight miles away, at Doncaster, the old London & North Eastern Railway; but here I was a schoolboy now in the British Railways era.

One of the most popular places for train-spotting was on the road from Mexborough to Wath upon Dearne, at a spot known locally as Wragby Row. Here you could watch two different railways, the old LMS and the old GCR at almost the same time, with the GCR running on a bottom line while diagonally across the bridge and the banking, ran the old LMS Railway.

On the bottom line was the route from Mexborough to Wath upon Dearne and Barnsley, with a junction to and from York. The lines were used mainly for freight trains and a large amount of light engine movements to and from Mexborough locomotive shed and the large marshalling yards at Wath upon Dearne. It was a common sight to see as many as five light engines coupled together, this being the maximum allowed, mostly of Classes 02, 04, or 'Austerity' freight engines. Apart from a few passenger trains to and from Doncaster and Barnsley, there was little glamour, with one exception, and that was the highlight of the day, the York to Bournemouth express.

The train was hauled by a 2-6-2 Class V2 passenger engine, but the main interest was the rolling stock which was composed entirely of green Southern Region coaches. Just before 11.30 a.m. we all stood on a small bridge over the line from York to hear and then see the train thunder along below us and, after slowing for the junction, the beautiful sight of the Class V2 engine with about twelve coaches accelerating away through a steep cutting, where the sound of the engine would echo along the cutting walls.

On schooldays, with my school on the top of the cutting, I always found an excuse, every morning, to stand by the window just to watch the express train below, speeding towards its destination. The same express train, but now travelling in the reverse direction from Bournemouth to York used to return about 6 p.m. hauled by a 4-6-0 Class B1 engine and, although still a splendid sight, it did not have the impact of the morning train.

On the upper line ran the old LMS Railway and, of the two, this was the line with the local glamour, and I stood for hours watching the fast trains that were missing on the bottom lines.

The 'Thames Clyde' express, running between Glasgow and London (St. Pancras) and hauled by a 'Jubilee' class engine, was one of the named trains that passed and, with four sets of tracks plus the junction to and from York, there was always a wide variety of passenger and fast and slow freight traffic.

I had many an argument with my fellow train-spotters about the relative merits of the different lines and engines. They said that the main line was the LMS from Euston to Glasgow with its 'Royal Scot' and 'Princess Royal' class engines but, to me, the main line was a few miles away, the Great Northern, with the Class A4, A3, and A1 type engines.

However, I retained some loyalty to the bottom section of lines, referred to by my fellow train-spotters as only an old GCR branch line. The reason for my loyalty was simple; my father was a Mexborough guard who worked that line. My friends' fathers worked mainly at the local collieries or steelworks and earnt a lot more money there, but when my father's train passed, and he waved to me standing on the bank, I was the proudest lad there.

Another favourite haunt was Mexborough Station but, as it was about a mile away from home, I did not go there as often as I would have wished. The passenger train service was between Doncaster and Sheffield, and Doncaster and Barnsley, with a few cross-country services such as the Hull to Liverpool express hauled by Class B1 engines. There was also the usual freight workings and, with large carriage sidings and a yard there, something was always on the move.

As I grew older I travelled further afield, and my favourite place to visit was Doncaster Station. Along with dozens of other train-spotters I stood and watched with fascination all the great named express trains roaring through. One of these was the world famous 'Flying Scotsman', the 10 a.m. King's Cross to Edinburgh train, which passed through at about 12.40 p.m. with a scheduled time of 163 minutes to cover the 156 miles from London to Doncaster, hauled by a Class A4 Pacific locomotive. We all watched closely to see if today it was the turn of *Mallard*, which was built in 1935 at Doncaster and, in 1938, set the world speed record for steam locomotion at 126 m.p.h., a record that still stands today, but although I saw *Mallard* dozens of times, it was never at the head of the 'Flying Scotsman'.

When I and my fellow train-spotters were on a back platform trying to beg a chance just to stand on a footplate, or touch a nameplate, we were all told of the approaching express by other spotters, and if a Class A4 locomotive was approaching the shout of Streak, so nicknamed because of its shape, would echo along the station, and lads would appear from nowhere as if by magic just to savour the magnificent engine roaring non-stop through the station.

Other trains also seen included the 'Yorkshire Pullman' the 'Tees-Tyne Pullman' and the 'White Rose', which all passed Doncaster and were a dream for all lovers of fine engines and luxury travel.

If a Class B1 engine hauled a passenger train to Mexborough, it received some attention but, at Doncaster, it was hardly noticed amongst the named engines.

The highlight of my schooldays was the twice a year trip to see my relations in London, when I could travel behind one of the great engines on the main line between Doncaster and King's Cross. After a sleepless night through excitement the great moment came, at last, when I stood on Doncaster Station waiting for the southbound train.

I always hoped for Class A4 although the engine was usually either a Class A3 or A1 Pacific. However, as long as it had a name, that was all that mattered. Once or twice to my horror I had to travel behind an unnamed Class V2. The journey was spent going from one window to another just to see more engines, more signal boxes, and to soak up all the atmosphere of a steam train journey, taking details of the trip to tell all my envious friends on my return.

With my father being a guard, I longed to accompany him but, of course, with railway rules to consider, that was out of the question, although I could try and find a way around the problem. After a great deal of thought, I found the answer.

Every September, there is a large race meeting held at Doncaster, and many local freight train crews were called in to work the race special excursion passenger trains. My father was one of the men involved so I simply went to Mexborough Station and bought a return ticket to Doncaster. The trains were always full so I could not get a seat, even if I had wanted one, so I had to stand up in the guard's van. It worked perfectly, and I was not breaking any railway regulations. It was a joy to be allowed to sit in the guard's seat and watch the vacuum guage, and to have signal boxes and junctions pointed out, to be recorded in the log.

Instead of going to the races I just spent the afternoon watching the trains, before returning home on the same train. I could not make the trips very often as it would have meant absence from school, but I considered the occasional 'truant' well worthwhile.

After one of these trips out, my father had a few days holiday and, before starting back to work, he had to enquire what his next turn of duty would be, and he asked me to accompany him to the railway. I expected to go to the guard's room at the traffic office but, instead, we went to the local shunting yard, known as the 'top yard', so he could telephone in. I stood near the entrance watching the freight trains shunting while he went into the small Mexborough No. 4 signal box and, after a few minutes, he shouted to me to join him. With great excitement I went into my first signal box.

My father had asked permission for me to enter the box and, because it was only a siding box, and not on the main line, permission had been given. I ran up the steps of the signal box, thrilled to enter a new exciting world. I stood just inside the door taking in the small neat row of levers, the block indicators, the diagram above the levers, the small neat cabin full of a wonderful sight, and the smell from the paraffin hand-lamp and polish. After a few minutes, I bravely walked around the box asking question after question. The signalman was very friendly and answered all my questions; then came a moment I will never forget.

The signalman moved a lever then he asked me to do the same and,

11

after careful instruction, I pulled over my first lever. It was painted white, which meant it was only a spare lever and not coupled to anything, but I did not know this until much later when, as a train register boy, I learnt the trade. I was overjoyed and, in that short space of time, I had already decided I was going to be a signalman. I did not know how, when or where, but my mind was made up, I was going to work on the railway.

# Chapter Two
# First Steps

The letter arrived in reply to my application for employment with British Railways. Every morning I had met the postman, and it seemed that I had been waiting months when, in actual fact, it had been only a few days, so hastily I ripped open the envelope but then, for a second, I stopped to think. I wanted to be a railwayman but what if now this denied me that chance. My doubts only lasted a few seconds because there, before my eyes, was the wonderful news.

I had to go for a medical prior to employment. I rushed inside the house wildly excited with my news, only to be brought back to earth with a bang. My parents told me that this was only the first step and not to take things for granted but, with a smile, they wished me the best of luck. I read the letter again and again, along with the free travel pass to Doncaster in a few days time.

I checked the times of the trains many times but, when the actual day arrived, I was still at the station half an hour before time. One long loud ring from the platform bell signified the train's arrival and, almost before it had stopped, I was climbing aboard. After the normal two minutes of station duties, the train slowly moved away, and I sat down in an empty compartment feeling a little nervous and frightened at the thought of what lay ahead. Just before reaching Doncaster, I went to the mirror to comb my hair in order to look my best for the medical officer when, to my horror, I saw dirty marks all over my face, caused from looking out of the train window and getting a face full of the steam engine's coal dust and smoke. I was panic-stricken, as here I was, only minutes away from the most important meeting in my life, looking, as they say in Yorkshire, 'a right scruff'. I dashed to the toilet for the quickest wash I can remember. Time was running out and the train had now stopped; but outside the station.

Was I going to be late? Why didn't I catch an earlier train? These were the thoughts that rushed through my head but, after what seemed an eternity, the train slowly started moving, to arrive only five minutes late. I knew the layout of the station, so I set off quickly to try and regain the lost time, arriving slightly breathless, but on time. I was shown to a waiting-room already occupied by some other lads about my age, and they also all looked nervous, so I unsuccessfully tried to reassure myself by thinking it was only a medical.

'Mr Newbould please' came the request from the office. The moment of truth had arrived and I meekly followed the attendant into the doctor's office. I had to undergo several tests with the main test being eyesight, and then I was told to dress as the examination was over. I must have looked worried as the doctor told me that I would be notified of the result, but his friendly nod gave me reason to feel happy about the outcome. I then strolled out of his office on top of the world and back to the station

E. J. STEPHENS
*District Operating Superintendent*
Telephone
DONCASTER 4031
Ext. 64
Our Reference S2/-
Your Reference –

DISTRICT OPERATING SUPT.
EASTERN REGION
ST. JAMES' BRIDGE
DONCASTER

19th March, 1956.

Mr D.A. Newbould,
9 Cambridge Street,
MEXBOROUGH.

Dear Sir,
    Referring to your application for employment.

    You have passed a satisfactory entrance medical examination
on the 15th instant and I am prepared to give you a trial as Telegraph
Lad Rest Day Relief at Mexborough and you may report to the Station
Master at Mexborough for duty as soon as convenient. Will you please
advise me when you will do so.

    Your rate of pay will be 66/6d. per week. You must distinctly
understand that your retention will depend upon you conducting yourself
and performing your duties in a satisfactory manner and being found
otherwise suitable.

    I shall require a sight of your birth certificate and your
school report. Will you please hand these to the Station Master.

Yours faithfully,

E. J. Stephens
District Operating Superintendent.

---

for the return home, feeling very grown-up at the thought of starting
work, so instead of just train-spotting on the return journey I decided to
look at this stretch of line.

The first section from Doncaster to Mexborough was opened around
1849 and, in 1871, was extended to Sheffield. The line is still a tribute to
the skill of the old railway builders because, after leaving the maze of

14

tracks in Doncaster the line goes through a very impressive cutting between Hexthorpe and Warmsworth, with the cutting sides over 70 ft. high in places, and then it passes through Conisbrough Tunnel. Beyond the tunnel, one can see a magnificent view of the railway viaduct proudly standing across the valley, carrying the old Dearne Valley Railway. After a good view of Conisbrough Castle, the line passes the buildings and headgear of Cadeby and Denaby collieries, part of the industrial scenery so much in evidence in this area, before arriving at Mexborough.

A letter arrived a few days later, with the good news that I had passed the examination, and that I was now a railwayman. The letter read; 'You have passed a satisfactory entrance medical examination and I am prepared to give you a trial as telegraph lad rest day relief at Mexborough, and you may report to the stationmaster for duty as soon as is convenient. The rate of pay is £3 6s. 6d. per week'. After a quick word to my parents, I was off to see the stationmaster to arrange to start. I had a short interview, and was told to report at 9 a.m. Monday next, for duty. My first step towards a railway career had arrived.

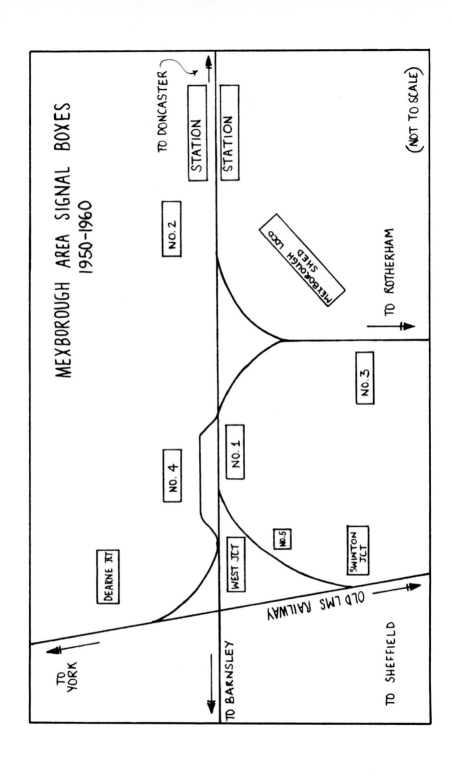

MEXBOROUGH AREA SIGNAL BOXES
1950-1960

TO DONCASTER

STATION

STATION

NO. 2

MEXBOROUGH SHED LOCO

TO ROTHERHAM

NO. 3

NO. 4

NO. 1

DEARNE JCT

WEST JCT

NO.5

SWINTON JCT

OLD LMS RAILWAY

TO YORK

TO BARNSLEY

TO SHEFFIELD

(NOT TO SCALE)

# Chapter Three
# Train Register Boy

My first day was a big disappointment. After my visit to the office a guard walked with me to Mexborough No. 3 signal box, not to show me where the box was, but to act as a guide as we crossed two sets of running lines. I was introduced to the signalman as 'Young Newbould' and my first instructions, very simple and straightforward, were to sit down on a locker out of the way, keep quiet, and listen to the bell codes.

After an hour, I was still sitting there, unable to tell which bell was which because, to my untrained ear, they all sounded the same, or why a bell was quiet or ringing. Also, I was totally unable to follow anything that was happening. What a start to a career I thought.

It was a help knowing the area and, with the aid of the signal box diagram I knew that No. 3 was not only a busy junction, but the only entrance and exit to Mexborough locomotive sheds, and the entrance box to the Rotherham and Sheffield area via the old GCR branch line. I was given a copy of the bell signals to read and then, during a quieter moment, the signalman briefly told me about the sequence of bells and signals, giving me my first lesson on signalling. Although I found it all very fascinating, it was at the same time bewildering.

Mexborough No. 3 signal box was a favourite for the training of new lads because it was the smallest box and with only fifty levers and only

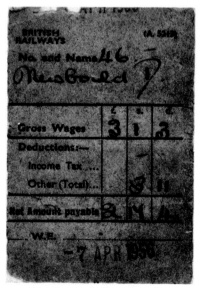

The Author's first pay slip.

four block bells, it was the easiest box in which to understand all the strange bell codes. I went home still very puzzled but happy, looking forward to the next day when I would learn more about my new trade.

With an upbringing in a railway environment, and with my hobby of train-spotting, it all helped me to learn. I knew, by the engine head-lamps, the class of train so I only had to translate the class to the bell code. A class A express passenger train was signalled by 4 bells consecutively, a class B ordinary passenger train by 3 +1, and a class G light engine by 2 +3. After a few days I had progressed enough to read the most popular bell codes.

My next task was to sit at the side of the regular train register boy to learn how to record all the bell signals in the train register book, as a written record had to be made of all bell signals with the exact time. The lad's duties also included the answering of the telephones and the relaying of information to the signalman, including such details as what passenger trains passed stations or select passing points and what engine was ready to depart from Mexborough Shed, and to forward train information further down the line. All trains had a working timetable number or a special number so a message would be 797 for a York to Sheffield goods train, followed by a light engine for Darnall Shed.

I fully realized I knew nothing about signalling regulations, special instructions, traffic regulations, point to point running times, control work or the many other details a signalman has to know and fully understand but, as with any apprenticeship, I had five years to learn. Everyone employed on British Railways is issued with the rule book, which he must thoroughly learn and know, as it covers all aspects of railway work. I found it interesting, but as there were 239 rules to read and study, it was rather a slow task and, to the average man in the street, it would be as interesting to read as a telephone directory, but if I wanted to be a signalman I had to read and learn it.

After a few more weeks of training I knew enough to cover the lads' duties at No. 3 box, and as I was on rest day relief I was moved to No. 2 box and then to No. 1 box. The signalmen at all the boxes, after my training, all said that I was competent as a train register boy so I was given my duties for the following week. No one under sixteen years of age could work on the night shift, so my turns of duty were either 6 a.m. to 2 p.m. or 2 p.m. to 10 p.m. A typical weekly rota would include Monday, 6 a.m. No. 1 box, Tuesday, 6 a.m. No. 3 box, Wednesday, 6 a.m. No. 2 box, Thursday, 2 p.m. No. 3 box, Friday, 2 p.m. No. 1 box and Saturday, 2 p.m. No. 2 box.

With a triangle of railways at Mexborough, all the three signal boxes with train register boys were within a short walking distance of one another, and working with nine different regular signalmen plus two rest day relief signalmen and relief signalmen to cover for holidays and sickness, my railway education started.

I was on duty a few days after completing my training at No. 2 box near the station with a signalman named Jack Hewitt. I had not met him before as he had been away, but I had been told about his quiet manner although, after a few minutes, I realized that a joke had been played on me. A stationary freight train was blocking the junction while waiting

18

for crew relief and in danger of delaying a passenger train, and a local set of Mexborough men were just strolling towards it, so Jack opened the window and turned the air blue. I thought I had heard some bad language before but nothing like this. However, it worked, because the train crew now rushed to the train and were quickly away and clear of the junction.

Jack came back from the window, smiling all over his face, saying to me 'That got the ...... train moving'. Then he realized that I was a new young lad and he thought about apologizing but, talking to himself, he said that I had to get used to the language sooner or later. Rumour had it that apart from the passengers on the station, people in the market place nearly a quarter of a mile away all knew when he was on duty due to his loud and colourful expressions, but I found Jack to be very friendly and helpful.

In the signal box the signalman was the captain of the ship, his word was law, and the lads had to do what he said. The other two men at No. 2 box were very strict and the only conversation was strictly work, with 'Has the 'up' passenger train left Rotherham', or 'what's the next 'down' freight train in the goods line' being the only type of conversation used. All the lads in the boxes were kept on a very tight rein but, at the end of the day, with a keen and conscientious signalman, their skill and knowledge was passed on.

My training was increasing daily because at No. 2 box, on the goods lines to and from No. 1 box, and in the other direction to and from Denaby Crossing box, the permissive block system was used. It is for freight trains only, to permit more than one train to be in a block section, on the same line, at the same time. I found out that there was a passenger and platform permissive block system, but, as it was not applicable in the Mexborough area, I did not get to study it, deciding that I would have time to do this later.

I learnt the tricks of the trade which assisted both enginemen and signalmen alike; tricks brought about from years of experience and not found in the rule books. With busy junctions it is a continuous jigsaw puzzle trying to move as many trains as possible in the quickest time possible, all while keeping within the safety rules and regulations. With passenger trains mixed on the same lines as freight trains, it was a work of art getting the freight trains clear of the passenger trains, to avoid delays to the latter.

In any industrial area, one of the main problems, and the railwayman's worst enemy, is foggy weather or falling snow, and with Mexborough, already shrouded in smoke both from industry and the engine shed, plus the river and canal nearby, it had more than its share of fog. One tip I learnt that was helpful to a driver was the use of verbal information. A train crew relief cabin was situated just outside No. 2 box connected by a loudspeaker from box to cabin and the signalman, after informing the train crew of their approaching train in fog, also informed them of the positions of the signals in advance.

Another helpful move concerned freight trains not having crew relief, but about to enter goods lines already occupied by other trains. The signalman stood at the window and either shouted or held up the appropriate number of fingers to the driver. It indicated to him how many trains were in front, so the driver then had a good idea as to how much line would be clear before reaching the other trains, and it helped everybody by keeping the trains moving just a bit quicker.

I found Mexborough No. 1 signal box of interest as it had more block bells to the other boxes, because while No. 2 and No. 3 boxes only worked to three other boxes No. 1 box worked to six other boxes. These included Swinton Junction, Mexborough West Junction Nos. 4, 3 and 2 and, in the middle of the day, Mexborough No. 5 box. It was only opened for a ground frame into Dale Browns Works, for the daily working of the pilot to move the wagons of sand in to the glassworks. At 3.30 p.m., No. 5 box closed, which gave me a chance to learn about Block Regulation No. 24 (opening and closing of signal boxes). When box No. 5 was switched out, Swinton Junction was worked to, and as it was a box on the old LMS, it still used the LMS method of block telegraph. This was slightly different with its 'train on line' and 'train out of section' signals, but it all increased my knowledge.

A year quickly passed as I covered the three boxes, and reached the age of sixteen. I was now, by law, allowed to work the night duty, so I could now apply for a regular train register boy position with one signalman and, as a vacancy had occurred at No. 3 box, I applied, with success. I had an affection for No. 3 box as it was the first one I had worked in, and Signalman Fred Brooks was the man who gave me my first lessons in the trade. At last, one very small step up the ladder had been made.

After a year of working on two shifts a week, I felt very much grown-up because, on the following Monday, I started work at 10 p.m. on my very first night turn of duty.

At 2 a.m. in the morning, instead of feeling tired, I was still full of life and very much awake, happy to be seeing some different trains. One train that stood out passed at 2.45 a.m., this being the first passenger train of the day, a newspaper train from Doncaster to Sheffield. I saw the Class B1 engine coming around the corner with its two electric headlights beaming, the big black engine throwing out a shower of sparks as it passed the box and disappeared into the darkness. The locomotive shed came to life around 4 a.m. with a flood of prepared engines moving to the turntable, and all the bustle associated with the start to another day. The last two hours were very hectic and, at 6 a.m., I suddenly felt tired and sleepy, so I went home to bed after a very happy first night shift.

On a steam engine, the driver allows the fireman to drive at certain times to gain experience and to learn his trade, and a similar situation applied in the signal box. Rule No. 71 states that train register boys or other unauthorized persons must not be allowed to work signals, points, train signalling instruments, bells or gongs, but a signalman would use his vast experience to judge when his train register boy was ready and, over a long period of time, he would let his lad use the levers and bells. However, I must stress that this was always under very strict supervision.

To further my education on railways I attended night-school classes for train signalling, and I still have my certificates. My mate Fred would spend hours teaching me all about the rules and regulations and, because a large amount of the regulations were used only in an emergency, we used to invent fictitious situations, and I would have to solve the problem. For this I cannot thank him enough and credit should also go to the many other signalmen who do the same because, without their help and guidance, there would not be trained and keen train register boys to follow in their shoes.

Apart from recording all the bell signals in the train register book, I also had to spend a great deal of time on the telephone. One line was from Mexborough locomotive top pit cabins, so engines leaving the shed there reported to the box, while another line was a local yard telephone. Then there was the most-used telephone, the Mexborough to Rotherham circuit, where up to nine signal boxes would all be switched into the same open circuit, all having their own call sign.

The calls that I had to send were 'down' circuit calls in which I gave the train details and, in the case of passenger or a fully-fitted fast freight, the time of passing for example, the 181 express passing at 11.27 a.m. followed by 797 York to Sheffield freight.

One morning I made a mistake and reported the trains the wrong way round and, after saying the Wath to Toton freight first, there was an uproar from 'Little Jim', the signalman at Greasbrough Road box further down the line near Rotherham. He shouted, 'We have two freight trains in the 'down' goods loop, another one shunted at Aldwalke, another one up the bank at Thrybergh Junction, and you let another freight train run in front of the express, without anywhere to shunt it, and without running time'. As he was responsible for the regulation of the freight trains after Rotherham he had a right to be upset, as he would have to run a train out of the goods loop to make room for the following train, causing even more delay to the express. Fortunately, he calmed down as I explained my error, but I must admit to a few more mistakes made on purpose after that, just to upset him.

Another trick on the same theme required the help of the signalman at Thrybergh Junction, Peter Ladley, who would ask in no uncertain terms what the freight train was when he already knew what was coming, having received the bell code for the passenger train.

Saturday night at 10 p.m. is not a very good time for a lad in his teens to go to work when all mates are out having fun, but after a few minutes spent on the circuit phone I felt a lot happier, because all the signalmen and train register boys were a load of laughs. If a signalman admitted to doing something foolish at home he would have his leg pulled for days. One example was of a signalman who travelled miles to buy a cheap garage, only to find when he arrived there that the firm who sold them had gone. He subsequently had dozens of calls asking if he knew anywhere that sold cheap garages.

The Saturday afternoon turn of duty was not popular, because it was the shift during which the lads had to clean all the signal box windows, polish the lever handles and do all the cleaning jobs that were required, this being part of the job. During one such Saturday, the signalman, Fred, who answered the telephones if I was busy or absent, told me I was required on the circuit phone. It was the signalman at Rotherham (Central) box who had someone there to talk to me; his daughter.

I have a shy nature, and knowing that at least six signalmen were listening but keeping quiet, it was a short and difficult conversation. Later on in the shift I was asked by the signalman to visit his home for my Sunday tea, and to meet his daughter. Now I had a problem, in that I had to decide whether it a serious request or if I was to be the next victim for a leg pull. In the end, I decided to call everyone's bluff by saying I would be delighted to go. The following day I did just that, thinking if nobody met me off the bus I would deny going at all; but it was genuine. On the next day back at work I was asked about my visit. I replied that I was not going to fall for that trick and, after a couple of days, the incident was forgotten, but as I continued visiting for a long time after that, I felt the joke was on the others.

Mexborough No. 3 box had some unusual signals. Between No. 1 and No. 3 boxes there must be one of the shortest block sections on the railway as from No. 1 starter signal to No. 3 home signal, there was only room for two light engines to stand. The reason for this was that a light engine would be clear of both junctions and, with so many light engines returning back to Mexborough Shed, it helped the traffic flow.

Another feature at No. 3 box was a distant signal in advance of the box, and the only reason I could find for this was that it showed an engine driver coming off the shed that the 'down' starter signal was off, as he was joining a running line and not getting the normal distant signal.

On the 'up' main line, between Mexborough No. 3 and No. 1 boxes, there was a permanent speed restriction of 15 m.p.h. because of a curve over the canal, a road bridge and an uphill gradient. It was very hard for a driver with a full load on to get his train round the curve without stopping, as he had to go so slow uphill.

After learning the rules and regulations I was, at times, working the box under supervision. Despite this, I was still short on experience and at 3 a.m. one Sunday morning, I learnt an important lesson; to always think in advance.

At that early hour, traffic was light, so when the Locomotive Shed Foreman telephoned that an engine off Mexborough Shed was to proceed light to Wath Yard, I got off my chair to send the engine forward to Mexborough No. 1 box. My mate had a quick glance at the clock and told me to let the engine stop where it was.

A passenger service called the 'Starlight Special' ran with cut price tickets between London and Scotland, in both directions on Fridays and Saturdays throughout the summer. These trains were routed from Marylebone, via Leicester and York, to Scotland. I knew the express was due to pass in fifteen minutes but the light engine would have cleared West Junction, with time to spare before the express turned off at the junction, but the order had been given so I sat down again slightly puzzled.

The express slowly passed with a long and crowded train and, because of the gradient and the speed restriction, it stopped and stuck in the section, with the driver sounding the engine's whistle for assistance. Fred sent the light engine into the section to act as a banker and, after a few moments, the express train was assisted off the curve and sent on its way without undue delay. I now realized that the light engine had been held back in anticipation of such an event happening, for although the curve was close to the locomotive shed, it might have been quite a while before an engine would have been ready to assist.

I had just seen a very smart piece of good railway work by a signalman, and, if there was nothing to show for it on paper, at least the train crew knew its value.

Mexborough No. 3 box had a 'down' loop line which could hold a freight train of up to 65 wagons, and it was used for higher class trains to pass. It saved having a train stood at either junction home signal because, as the boxes were so close, unless the train was very short, it would stand foul at the junction at the rear.

The line was one of the few passenger loops, and it was used on Sunday evenings in the summer season for returning coastal excursions terminating at Rotherham (Central) Station, which required not only time for departing passengers to alight but for the train engine to run round the empty stock before moving it clear of the station.

One day I was asked to see the stationmaster who asked, during the interview, if I would work as a shunter as there was a severe shortage of suitable men. Apart from the experience I would gain, I would also be paid twice the wages I now received and at eighteen and a half years of age, that was enough incentive. I was now on adult wages and when I was twenty I had a choice of either stopping as a shunter, train to be a guard like my father, or go back to the box as a signalman. Until I made up my mind I moved outside, to become a junior relief shunter; another step up the ladder.

# Chapter Four
# Signalman's Training

I did not enjoy work as a shunter. After the luxury of a clean warm signal box, I did not take kindly to the weather, the dirty conditions and the danger. I was back on relief duties again and I worked at two yards at Mexborough and one at Aldwalke, near Rotherham, each one very different from the other.

Mexborough No. 2 Yard handled both passenger stock and freight work, and there were six carriage sidings, plus three more at the rear of the station for the coaching stock. In addition, there were five sidings known as Sheffield Sidings for the freight traffic. On the passenger side, on Sundays during the summer season, there was coaching stock to prepare for trains from either Mexborough, Bolton upon Dearne, or Rotherham to Cleethorpes, Scarborough, Bridlington, Blackpool and other coastal resorts.

At other days throughout the year there were coaches for football specials and special excursions to the more popular centres; London being the favourite destination.

I learnt about buckeye coupling, vacuum-pipes, heating pipes, vestibule shields and how to climb under, over and on top of coaches, but in the winter it was cold and dirty, and it was hard work. The engines for the special trains were usually from Mexborough Shed, and included Class B1 locomotives Nos. 61166, 61167, 61168, 61169 and 61194, and all were turned out looking very clean. Not a large amount of freight was shunted, and I even moved the pilot engine No. 64377 within the sidings while learning more about enginemen and local freight workings.

Mexborough Top Yard was strictly freight and incorporated eight main sidings, and on arrival, a freight train would be shunted into a long empty siding to clear the goods line. The train engine would then be despatched either to the shed or to its return working. The yard pilot engine would then go on to the train and pull it up a goods spur line towards West Junction, then shunt the wagons back towards the various sidings.

The head shunter would uncouple the wagons, and signal to the shunters or chasers which siding the wagon had to enter. This signalling was done by a strange hand or arm code, which was easy to follow after a while. Here are a few examples of the code.

| No. 3 Sidings | Circular motion with one hand |
| No. 6 Sidings | Circular motion with two hands |
| No. 7 Sidings | Hitting right thigh with right hand |
| Back line sidings | Arm across chest |

As junior shunters we would watch the signals and, a hand lamp was used at night or in bad weather. We would move the point levers to the correct sidings and then chase the wagons, slowing them down with a brake stick on the brake lever, then run back up the siding to read the next signal. With a rake that would travel back towards you at great speed, you had to be quick and alert, as a 16 ton coal wagon was not something to treat lightly and in bad weather, extra care was needed.

A team of three did the chasing, but we were all young and somehow managed to keep out of each other's way and also keep the wagons moving, mostly into the correct siding. There was a road bridge right over the yard, and I often wondered what a stranger walking past thought about the hand signals and all the running about.

One very dark, wet and windy night was very nearly my last. The head shunter had sent two of us down to No. 1 Siding to prepare a partly-fitted freight train from Mexborough to Annesley, near Nottingham, and we had to couple up all the wagons and connect the vacuum-pipes to the front few wagons, prior to the train's departure. We both knew the train engine would not be very long before it arrived, so my mate walked to the front of the train to stop the engine short of the wagons while I was working underneath.

With a large amount of freight train movement up and down on the next set of lines, and with the wind howling, it was very difficult to hear when the engine would arrive, but I was not worried as my mate would protect me. The next thing I knew was a voice shouting 'stop' and, looking underneath through the wagons, I could see the engine wheels stopping. The voice was that of the fireman who was guiding the steam engine back and, luckily for me, the experience of the driver by stopping short of the train had saved me because, if the wagons had moved, I could have been trapped either under the wheels or between the buffers.

The train crew could not see my hand lamp, as I was holding it up so that I could see to fasten the vacuum-pipe. I climbed out quickly from under the wagons feeling very shaken to find out why my mate had not stopped the engine and I saw him over the other side of the yard standing under cover out of the rain, unaware of what had nearly happened.

I was livid, and if I could have reached him just then I would have hit him with my brake stick for being so foolish, but the train crew made me calm down and carry on working so the train could leave on time. In the cabin afterwards I was still angry, so the head shunter gave the other shunter a proper roasting followed by a lecture on safety and danger to others and, for a long time afterwards, the atmosphere was very strained.

The other yard at Aldwalke I enjoyed, as the shunting duties were very small and I could spend nearly all my time in the signalbox. I knew all the signalmen there, and as they were working twelve hours a day they were all glad of the extra help and, as I was still going to night school for signalling classes, I was able to keep in touch with the job I really wanted; that of a signalman.

One amusing incident happened there when a freight train passed the box to go across the road back into the sidings. The fireman's food fell out of his bag and on to the ballast and, as the train came back on the other line, he climbed off the engine to come to the box to make the tea. He saw the packet of food on the floor and promptly kicked it down the bank into a muddy stream. I could not stop laughing, as his face was a picture when he realized what he had done.

I reported for duty at 6 a.m. one Monday morning at Mexborough Top Yard and, as usual, went into No. 4 signal box to talk to the signalman. It was here I was asked to go on to the private telephone line to No. 1 box to be told the sad news that over the weekend, Fred, my old signalman mate and friend at No. 3 box had died. I was very upset because having worked as a team you grew very close, and we had a very good working relationship.

A large number of signalmen at these busy signal boxes did not reach retiring age, partly because of the long hours they had to work. After a full week on night duty from Monday to Saturday they came back at 6 p.m. on Sunday evening to work until 6 a.m. Monday morning and, after going home to have a meal and snatch a few hours sleep, then it was back again at 2 p.m. until 10 p.m. for another week. On the Saturday, they would double back to work at 6 a.m. Sunday morning for a twelve hour shift, and then work from 6 a.m. to 2 p.m. for the rest of the week. Apart from a rest day and one Sunday off every three weeks, they lived at work as the bank holidays were all working days and, apart from the two weeks annual holiday, that was all the time they had off.

The hard physical work of pulling heavy levers, and the mental strain in trying to keep all the traffic moving in all weathers, as well as not having a proper meal break, all took its toll. The railway did not stop running while a signalman stopped for a meal, and it was no joke trying to eat a sandwich and pull a lever at the same time.

After the funeral I decided I was going back as a signalman as soon as I could, so that all the training Fred had given me would not have been in vain.

I called at the Traffic Office at Mexborough to collect my pay packet and I was handed a letter dated 23rd March 1961, one day after my twentieth birthday. It was the letter I was waiting for and it read 'Training as signalman'. 'Please arrange to report to the Signalling School, at Doncaster, for the course commencing at 9 a.m. Monday, 27th March 1961. The course is from Monday to Friday each week, with four hours practical training at Kilnhurst Central Station signal box every Saturday morning'. Apart from myself, two more train register boys from Mexborough went back to school to join up with about two dozen new trainees.

We were split up in to two groups. My group were all ex-train register boys with a good knowledge of the job, but the other group were from jobs outside the railway and most of them had never even been inside a signal box. Thinking back five years, I could remember my feelings when I started, and I felt sorry for these lads, especially the ones with no railway background or, more importantly, no interest, as they would soon lose heart and not last the course.

The school was set up with bells and block instruments the same as a working signal box, and the ex-train register boys looked forward to the course as a means of getting away from shift working and to having a few weeks on a 9 to 5 turn of duty. We were all taught the regulations for Train Signalling on Double Lines by the Absolute Block System, the

**BELL SIGNALS**

| See Regulation | Class of Train | Description | Code |
|---|---|---|---|
| APPLICABLE — | | TO ALL REGIONS<br>Call Attention | 1 |
| APPLICABLE | | TO ALL REGIONS EXCEPT SOUTHERN | |
| 1 and 4 | A | **Is line clear for:—**<br>Express passenger train, newspaper train, breakdown van train or snow plough going to clear the line, or light engine going to assist disabled train<br><br>Officers' Special train not requiring to stop in section | 4 consecutively |
| | | Electric express passenger train | 4–2 |
| | B | Ordinary passenger train, mixed train, or breakdown van train NOT going to clear line | 3–1 |
| | | Electric ordinary passenger train | 3–1–2 |
| | | Branch passenger train<br>(Where authorised) | 1–3 |
| | C | Parcels, fish, fruit, horse, livestock, meat, milk, pigeon or perishable train composed entirely of vehicles conforming to coaching stock requirements | 1–3–1 |
| | | Express freight, livestock, perishable or ballast train, pipe fitted throughout with the automatic brake operative on not less than half of the vehicles | 3–1–1 |
| | | Empty coaching stock train (not specially authorised to carry "A" headcode) | 2–2–1 |
| | | Electric empty coaching stock train | 2–2–1–2 |
| | D | Express freight, livestock, perishable or ballast train, partly fitted, with the automatic brake operative on not less than one third of the vehicles | 5 consecutively |

4

Bell Signal regulations.

28

**Bell Signals**—*continued*

| See Regula-tion | Class of Train | Description | Code |
|---|---|---|---|
| 1 and 4 | E | **Is line clear for:—**<br>Express freight, livestock, perishable or ballast train, partly fitted, with not less than four braked vehicles next to the engine and connected by the automatic brake pipe<br><br>Express freight, livestock, perishable or ballast train, with a limited load of vehicles NOT fitted with the automatic brake | 1–2–2 |
| | F | Express freight, livestock, perishable or ballast train, NOT fitted with the automatic brake | 3–2 |
| | G | Light engine or light engines coupled (See Regulation 3)<br><br>Engine with not more than two brake vans | 2–3<br><br>1–1–3 |
| | H | Through freight or ballast train, not running under class "C", "D", "E" or "F" headcode | 1–4 |
| | J | Mineral or empty wagon train | 4–1 |
| | K | Freight, mineral or ballast train, stopping at intermediate stations<br><br>Branch freight train (Where authorised) | 3 consecutively<br><br>1–2 |
| 1, 5 and 8 | K | Freight, ballast or Officers' Special train, requiring to stop in section | 2–2–3 |
| 1, 5 and 9 | — | Trolley requiring to go into or pass through tunnel | 2–1–2 |
| 1 | — | Train entering section | 2 consecutively |

**Bell Signals**—*continued*

| See Regulation | Description | Code |
|---|---|---|
| | | |
| **APPLICABLE TO ALL REGIONS** | | |
| 1 and 4 (Also Out-of-Gauge Instructions) | Train which can pass an out-of-gauge or exceptional load similarly signalled on the opposite or an adjoining line | 2–6–1 |
| | Train which cannot be allowed to pass an out-of-gauge load of any description on the opposite or an adjoining line between specified points | 2–6–2 |
| | Train which requires the opposite or an adjoining line to be blocked between specified points | 2–6–3 |
| | Opposite line, or an adjoining line used in the same or opposite direction, to be blocked for passage of train conveying out-of-gauge load | 1–2–6 |
| 1 | Train approaching (where authorised) | 1–2–1 |
| 2 | Cancelling | 3–5 |
| | Last train signalled incorrectly described | 5–3 |
| 5 | Warning Acceptance | 3–5–5 |
| | Line now clear in accordance with Regulation 4 for train to approach | 3–3–5 |
| 6 and 12 | Train out of section, or Obstruction Removed | 2–1 |
| 7 | Blocking back inside home signal | 2–4 |
| | Blocking back outside home signal | 3–3 |
| | Train or vehicles at a stand | 3–3–4 |
| **APPLICABLE TO ALL REGIONS EXCEPT SOUTHERN** | | |
| 10 | Engine assisting in rear of train | 2–2 |
| | Engine with one or two brake vans assisting in rear of train | 2–3–1 |

7

30

**Bell Signals**—*continued*

| See Regulation | Description | Code |
|---|---|---|
| **APPLICABLE TO ALL REGIONS** | | |
| 11 | Engine arrived | 2–1–3 |
| | Train drawn back clear of section | 3–2–3 |
| 12 | Obstruction Danger | 6 consecutively |
| 16 | Train an unusually long time in section | 6–2 |
| 17 and 20 | Stop and examine train | 7 consecutively |
| 19 | Train passed without tail lamp | 9 consecutively to box in advance; 4–5 to box in rear |
| 20 | Train divided | 5–5 |
| 21 | Shunt train for following train to pass | 1–5–5 |
| 22 | Train or vehicles running away in wrong direction | 2–5–5 |
| 23 | Train or vehicles running away in right direction | 4–5–5 |
| 24 | Opening of signal box | 5–5–5 |
| | Closing of signal box | 7–5–5 |
| | Closing of signal box where section signal is locked by the block | 5–5–7 |
| 26 | Testing block indicators and bells | 16 consecutively |
| 31 | Shunting into forward section | 3–3–2 |
| | Shunt withdrawn | 8 consecutively |
| 32 | Working in wrong direction | 2–3–3 |
| | Train clear of section | 5–2 |
| | Train withdrawn | 2–5 |
| Signalmen's General Instructions | Distant signal defective | 8–2 |
| | Home signal defective | 2–8 |

8

31

object of the Absolute Block signalling being to prevent more than one train being in a block section on the same line at the same time.

All trains have a class of train description and bell code, and these are listed below.

| Class of Train | Description of Train | Bell Code |
|---|---|---|
| A | Express Passenger Train | 4 |
| B | Ordinary Passenger Train | 3 + 1 |
| C | Parcels, Fish, Fruit, Meat Train | 1 + 3 + 1 |
| C | Express Freight Livestock Train | 3 + 1 + 1 |
| D | Express Freight Partly Fitted | 5 |
| F | Express Freight Not Fitted Train | 3 + 2 |
| G | Light Engine | 2 + 3 |
| J | Empty Wagon Train | 4 + 1 |

This is the order of preference in running; for example, a Class C train would go before a Class F train.

No signalman must permit a train to move out of his control, and into the next block section, until he has obtained permission in advance from the signalman in the next box. The offering and acceptance of trains between boxes is carried out by means of a bell code, sent on a single stroke bell circuit.

Each box is equipped with electro-magnetic block instruments and the needle may be moved to provide a visual confirmation of acceptance of a train. When a signalman accepts a train he moves the needle on the block instrument by the handle from its normal position to the 'is line clear' position, and this is shown in the other box. To illustrate what happens one should imagine that I am the signalman at Kilnhurst, the box in the rear is No. 3, and the box in advance is Thrybergh Junction.

No. 3 box        Kilnhurst        Thrybergh Junction

The signalman at No. 3 box rings the bell once; 'call attention'. It is acknowledged by me at Kilnhurst so No. 3 box sends, for example, the bell code 3 + 1 + 1 (express freight train). As my line is clear, I answer the signal and place the block instrument to the 'is line clear' position and then record the signal and the time in the train register book. After a few minutes, No. 3 box sends, without 'call attention', 2 bells meaning 'train entering section' which I must answer. Then I place the block needle to the 'train on line' position. I then 'call attention' to Thrybergh Junction, to send the train forward in the same manner as No. 3 box sent it to me.

After acceptance, and when the block needle is in position, I then pull off the proper signals to the 'clear' position to allow the train to proceed.

As the train approaches me I send 'train entering section' to Thrybergh, and when the train has passed me in order I then replace the signals back to 'caution' and 'danger' and 'call attention' to No. 3 box. When this is acknowledged I give the 'train out of section' signal of 2 + 1, which is also acknowledged. I then place the block needle back to normal, record the bell codes in the train register book and, after receiving the 'train out of section' signal from Thrybergh, the cycle is complete. Where sections are short or where fast trains are running the 'is line clear' signal would be sent forward at once, and before the 'train on line' signal was received. The same method is applied to all trains, except in certain circumstances such as fog or falling snow.

There are 32 regulations; the main ones being regulations 4 and 6, which are used for every train.

Regulation 4 is 'Line clear or giving permission for a train to approach'. Very briefly, the line must be clear for at least one quarter of a mile ahead of the home signal, and all points within that area must be placed in the proper position. On no account after accepting a train must anything else be allowed on the section until after the train has passed, or it is brought to a stand at the home signal, or the cancelling signal 3 + 5 has been received.

Regulation 6 is 'train out of section'; 2 + 1. This is sent when the train has passed, complete with tail lamp at least one quarter of a mile beyond the home signal, or if it has been shunted clear of the section.

In addition to the Absolute Block regulations which have all to be learnt perfectly, there are also the Regulations for Train Signalling by the Permissive Block System. The object of Permissive Block is to permit more than one train to be in a block section on the same line at the same time.

There are three types of Permissive working, these being goods lines normally used by freight trains, passenger lines used by both passenger trains and freight trains, with Permissive Block used for the freight; and platform lines serving platforms, and used by both passenger trains and freight trains, the Permissive being used for the passenger trains.

A signalman may also have to learn, depending on the box where he is going to work, 'Signalling on Single Lines by Electric Token', or 'Signalling on Single Lines by Absolute Block System with Train Staff or Ticket Working'.

If all that was not enough to study, you also learnt about the Signalman's General Instruction. These covered special workings at signal boxes, working during fog or falling snow, and the use of lever collars, which are placed on a lever to prevent the lever being moved. When not required they were kept on a spare lever or if used unofficially, they made very good egg cups.

In addition, there are special instructions to cover Out of Gauge Loads, Royal Trains, Single Line Working, The Rule Book, Sectional Appendix to Working Timetables, etc.

A signalman, if he is lucky, can spend years in the box and not use a large number of the regulations, but he must know them all. It is not surprising that a large number of budding signalmen do not pass through the school.

Signal boxes are graded to the number of bell signals, levers moved, crossing gates opened and shut, and the amount of work a signalman would perform on his turn of duty. A Class 4 box was the lowest grade, followed by a Class 3, Class 2, Class 1, Special Class A and then Special Class B. When a relief signalman worked several signal boxes he was graded one class higher than the boxes so, for example, a Class 1 signalman would work Class 2 or 3 grade boxes.

The course instructor was Inspector A. Legge, an ex-Special Class signalman who made his sessions with the pupils very interesting by

E.R.O. 51994
OP. **2.**

*Form referred to in Rule 183, clause (g).*

**LONDON MIDLAND AND SCOTTISH RAILWAY.**

( A supply of these Forms must
  be kept by each Driver. )

# WRONG LINE ORDER FORM **B.**
# DRIVER TO SIGNALMAN.

*To the Signalman at*........................................................
*signal box.*

Allow an assisting engine or breakdown van train to proceed in the wrong direction to my train, which is

stationary on the*..........................................................line

at............................................ I will not move my engine in any direction until the arrival of the assisting engine.

Catch points exist at ................................................

Signed..........................................................*Driver.*

Date................19....... Time issued..............m.

† Countersigned............................................................
*Signalman.*

at............................................signal box.

* *Insert name of line, for example, Up or Down
  Main, Fast, Slow or Goods.*

† *If necessary.*

Wrong Line Order Form (Green).

E.R.O. 51995

*Form referred to in Rule 183, clause (i).*

## London Midland and Scottish Railway.

( A supply of these forms must
be kept by each guard. )

# WRONG LINE ORDER FORM C.
# GUARD TO DRIVER.

*To Driver of Engine No.* ...............................

I authorise you to set back to the rear portion of your train.

Catch points exist at ..............................................

Signed .......................................... *Guard.*

Date ..........................19.... Time issued..........m.

∗ Countersigned...........................................
*Driver of engine assisting in rear.*

∗ Countersigned...........................................
*Signalman.*

at ...........................................signal box.

∗ *If necessary.*

Wrong Line Order Form (Beige).

stories of his own experiences. Most were true but some, I suspect, were fictitious; but all related to the regulations and, for his pupils, it made a very hard task just a little less boring.

I was pleased to have had experience in the box and at night school class as the training was hard but, after only four weeks, I passed the course and became a trained signalman. I was sent to Kilnhurst box (Class 3) and, at this point, had almost fulfilled my ambition.

Every signal box is different, each with its own special working instructions, different sounding block bells and train movements. Because of this, a new signalman in a low class box would spend three weeks in training, a week for each shift. On my third week, the District Operating Superintendent came to visit the box and asked me about my knowledge of the rules and regulations. He then proceeded to watch my every move as I worked the box on my own. I felt very lonely and was afraid I would make a mistake but, after a while, I forgot I was on trial and enjoyed myself. It was soon over, and I was then told that I had passed and I would be in charge from 6 a.m. Monday, 29th May 1961. I had done it, and I was now a signalman.

Kilnhurst signal box, complete with the author's scooter.

# Chapter Five
# Early Signalling Days

The alarm clock rang loud at 5 a.m. but I was already awake, and got out of bed quickly. I was determined I was not going to be late for duty on my first morning so I washed, dressed and grabbed my bag with my breakfast inside as quickly as I could. I started my scooter and rode it through the streets where people were already on the move because, even at that hour, life in an industrial area, where the majority of the workforce worked around the clock, never really stopped.

I rode through the station yard, then across the timber battens between the rails, and parked the scooter at the side of the box. The box looked small and of little importance, but to me it meant everything. I had made the grade. The box door key was left outside in a secret place, known only to men qualified to work the box, so I took the key, opened the door and went inside for my first shift.

The interior had a cool feeling so I acted as many a signalman had done before leaving my jacket on, and I put the kettle on. My next move was to read the train register book because if anything was wrong it would be recorded there. Fortunately the page was clear, so I signed on duty.

I telephoned the signalman at No. 3 box to ask if the line was clear so I could switch in circuit, and his reply was in the affirmative. The signals were still off because the box had been closed since 5.45 a.m. on Sunday morning, so I replaced the levers back in the frame to return the signals to normal. I then turned the handle on the block shelf to connect to both boxes, and sent the bell signal 5 +5 +5, 'opening of signal boxes'. I was now ready for my first train.

There was a telephone to the Control Office, mounted to the wall at the side of the desk with the train recording book on it, so I lifted the telephone off its hook and reported to the Section Controller at Sheffield Office that Kilnhurst box was now opened. He did not recognize my voice so he asked who I was and, after I explained, he wished me luck. I thought this was really a nice gesture, not only from a stranger but from an old railwayman to a very new railwayman, and very thoughtful at such an early hour.

My next tasks were to open my locker, make the tea and light the coal fire, after which I reached for the signalman's tool of his trade, his duster, which is always used when moving any levers. It made the pulling easier because as the handle moves it gives a better grip and, if your hands were wet or sweating, it prevented them slipping. It also kept the lever handles bright, and prevented rusting.

Kilnhurst signal box was one mile 494 yds. from Mexborough No. 3 box and 1,277 yds. from Thrybergh Junction, and a Class 3 box. Absolute Block was worked in both directions and, in addition to the normal bell codes, special routing bell signals were operative. On the 'down' line it was for trains for the Silverwood branch line at Thrybergh while on the 'up' line 1 bell was used for Mexborough No. 1 box, 2 bells for Mexborough No. 4 or Top Yard, 3 bells for Mexborough Shed and no route bell for trains to Mexborough No. 2 box. All the route signals were sent after the 'is line clear' signal was accepted. With two station platforms, two goods sidings off the 'down' line, a small private works siding, an 'up' goods loop which could hold trains with up to 98 wagons, and a crossover road, it was a small but interesting layout.

A sudden ring on the bell from Mexborough No. 3 box startled me for a second, and when I acknowledged it I was offered the 2 +3 bell signal for a light engine. As the line was clear I accepted, and then I passed the bell signal forward to Thrybergh Junction, who accepted and gave me a 'line clear' position on the block indicator. This was very important, for it was also a release for my starter signal. If the bell signal had been refused, and the needle was not moved, I could not release my signal. This was another feature to safeguard against mistakes.

The levers were all painted in different colours with stop signals being red, distant signals yellow, points black, locking bars for points green and spare levers white. The levers were all interlocking in the room below so they could only be pulled in a certain rotation, which prevented a distant signal coming off before the stop signal to which it applied.

To follow the sequence I pulled lever No. 2 ('down' main home signal) followed by lever No. 3 ('down' main starter signal) and finally, lever No. 1 ('down' main distant signal). In addition to the colour, the lever had a small plate attached to it about half-way down, giving all the details of what the lever worked, and what other levers were also required.

The light engine was en route from Mexborough Shed to Ickles Sidings near Rotherham, to work a slow freight train to Frodingham, near Scunthorpe.

An old engine driver once told me that they all remembered their first trip in command, and I found that the same also applied to signalmen in remembering the passage of their first train or, in my case, a light engine. I felt more relaxed now that my first signalling moves had been completed, and I grew in stature as time moved on and as more trains came and departed.

A signal box on or near a station has a control for a large bell on the instrument shelf and, when operated, rings the bell on the platform to give the station staff notice that a stopping passenger train is approaching. We rang the bell after receiving the 'train on line' signal from either box, and as I rang the bell for the first time for an 'up' passenger train, just before 7 a.m. on a quiet morning, I thought I would wake up the entire population of the nearby colliery village, because I rang it a little louder than normal, just to make sure the staff heard it all right. Another advantage of the bell was that it was an ideal way to call the stationmaster in an emergency, as he lived in the station house.

The passenger train left on the 'up' line and then the 'down' passenger service came and departed, to be followed by a light engine for my sidings to work a freight train of empty coal wagons to the nearby Silverwood Colliery. I now had to use the siding points for the first time, and deviate from the normal straight through running. The light engine stopped outside the box, clear of the points, so I placed the home signal back to 'danger', moved lever No. 8 (points to No. 1 Siding) and then pulled lever No. 4 for a dolly signal or, to give it the correct title, a ground secondary signal fixed at a low level to aid the driver. After the signal came off, the engine moved inside the sidings and clear of the main line.

My first hour had passed safely so I decided it was about time I became sociable by joining my fellow signalmen on the circuit phone. I was made very welcome as I was now a signalman and not just a train register boy, and it was also a comfort to know that if I needed help or advice, I had only to ask and it would be given.

I kept an eye on the sidings to see if the freight train was ready to depart, and I then saw the guard approaching the box, shouting 'Are you there Bobby?' The name of 'Bobby' for a signalman dates back to the years between 1835 and 1875 when trains were hand-signalled by constables along the lineside, and the name is still used today. I opened the window, and the Mexborough guard recognized me and said 'Good morning young Newbould; I see that you have made it. My train is ready for Silverwood Sidings with 32 empties on, and we will be back here for another train load later on in the morning, so have the kettle boiling or else I will report you to your father, and if you are half as good a railwayman as he is, you will be all right, but don't whittle as much'. I smiled back and promised I would not forget and, after checking with Mexborough No. 3 box that no other train was ready, I despatched the train forward.

The engine whistle sounded, as if to defy the stillness of the morning, as the driver acknowledged the signal off. A hiss of steam came from the engine as it creaked, and groaned, and moved slowly forward, the wheels slipping for a moment on the damp rails. I could see the fireman busy with his shovel, as the driver coaxed the power from the engine as it took the strain and the weight of the train, heavy as the wagon wheels had been stood over the weekend and were reluctant to move. The train was now gathering momentum, the smoke from the engine's chimney billowing across the open fields. The empty wagons were clattering across the points and the fishplates joining the rails together were moving up and down with the weight, until the train was clear of the sidings. I saw that the tail lamp was in position on the goods brake van and was satisfied that the train was in order as it hurried along up the hill towards its destination, leaving behind a silent countryside again.

One of the most interesting train movements at Kilnhurst was a train on the 'up' line for the 'down' side sidings. The train would proceed into the 'up' goods loop and the engine would then be detached to return on the facing road on the main line, before going back into the loop to the rear of the train. The whole train was then pulled back from the 'up' goods loop over the crossover road and on to the 'down' main line, and then it was shunted back into the 'down' sidings.

The complete manoeuvre took a long time and blocked both main lines, so I had to be very careful not to cause any delay to other higher class trains which was very difficult, particularly in the dark, or in fog or falling snow. Fortunately it was the summertime now and the latter two conditions would not prevail until later, when I had gained a little more knowledge.

My first week on the day shift passed and then I was on night duty, from 10 p.m. to 6 a.m., Monday to Saturday. I had not had any problems so I was feeling pretty competent and looking forward to the next week but, as it happened, it did not start very well at all.

Control rang shortly after 10 p.m. to tell me to put the next 'up' freight train into the goods loop for about half an hour, as the train's relief crew had not yet signed on duty at the Mexborough relief point further up the line. As the freight train passed I received some black looks from the enginemen, because they knew at that time of night there should be nothing of greater importance behind them and, as soon as the train had stopped in the loop, the fireman was on the telephone, to enquire why they were stood there.

I explained, but my story was not accepted. I was told to inform Control that they were already on overtime working and, if kept back, they would miss the last bus home. This message was reported to Control and I was told that both the enginemen and guard had over two hours normal working to do, so they would have to wait and work to instructions. When the fireman rang me back I passed Control's message on to him and with that, the telephone was promptly slammed down. I felt like 'pig in the middle', getting involved in an argument that was not of my making, but I was only working to my instructions.

The half an hour passed and then Control rang to inform me that I could despatch the train, as the train's relief crew were now on duty. This I did, although I thought that the fireman had been a little unjust in grumbling to me, but I just had to accept it as part of the job, and carried on working. On the following two nights the freight train was running later and so it had a main line run but, on the Thursday, it was early once more, and again Control told me to put the train in the goods loop to await relief. I checked and found out it was the same crew as Monday night so this time, when the fireman telephoned, I was ready for him. It was my turn to voice an opinion so, in no uncertain terms, I passed on the message and this time, nothing was said in return.

Every week, to each depot, station and signal box are sent special train notices, circulars and a vacancy list. One vacancy caught my eye which read; 'Vacancy 10341 Class 2 signalman, Kilnhurst Central Thrybergh Junction' and, as it was the signal box next up the line, and a class higher, I knew I should apply for the post. There were several things in my favour including knowledge of the local trains, local area and men I knew and had worked with, but I considered I was a little short on experience. Three months is not a long time as a signalman, but my application form for the position was sent in, more in hope than in anticipation of actually getting the job.

I received a letter from Mr F. Adams, the stationmaster, dated 5th July 1961, to say I had been selected for the position of signalman at Thrybergh Junction, but I would have to wait until the summer holiday season was over for a relief signalman to become available to cover my duties, or until the post was filled.

Railway work is full of surprises. I did not expect to move so soon at the start of my career and, while I was waiting, I took my two weeks summer holiday. I often wondered what it must have been like for a signalman years ago, because my grandmother had told me what she could remember of her father, who had been a signalman in the Doncaster area between 1880 and 1900. The working day was a twelve hour shift, six days a week, and Sunday was the only day off, during which they had to attend church or chapel or be fined if they did not. I read a letter dated 14th April 1897 which read; 'The Directors have agreed to extensions in the annual leave. Signalmen (Class 1) would now receive five days, Class 2 men, four days, and Class 3 men, three days'. It was interesting to read that there was also, at that time, two classes of goods guards, with the first class men getting six days holiday while second class men received five days.

Times have certainly improved, thank goodness, and times were about to alter for me because of my transfer to Thrybergh Junction. I set off full of hope and expectation with regards to what I would find but, at the same time, wondering whether I could handle a higher class of signal box. Time alone would tell.

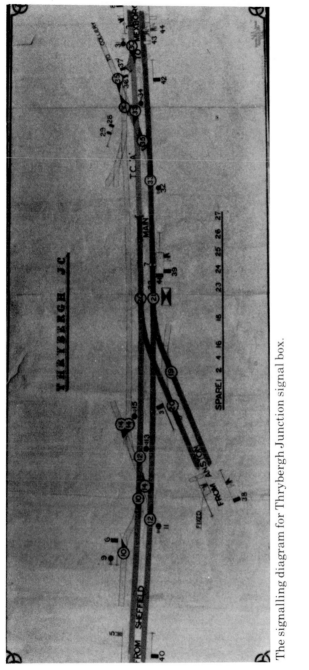

The signalling diagram for Thrybergh Junction signal box.

# Chapter Six
# The Runaway Train

Thrybergh Junction was a larger signal box, with 44 levers, and signalled to Kilnhurst, Aldwalke and Don Bridge. On the 'up' line there were three sets of sidings, the first set being Roundwood, where full trains, mostly from the Silverwood branch line, were shunted to be transferred to the old LMS Railway. Opposite the signal box were the yard sidings and further down the line, the colliery sidings, which were used very little.

On the 'down' line there was the junction to Don Bridge, the line then going to Silverwood Junction, Silverwood Sidings and through to Brancliffe East Junction, the few trains to work right over this line being freight only services to and from Worksop. The majority of trains to and from the junction were the local trip workings for Silverwood Colliery, and the three boxes were only open for two shifts, the late shift going home after the last trip train had departed.

The signal boxes were worked by signalwomen and were kept beautiful, more like a home than a place of work, and were a credit to the women, who must have spent hours keeping the boxes in this condition, even down to a bunch of flowers on the table.

The junction was also used as a shunting point for slow 'down' freight trains to clear a path for passenger trains and fast-fitted freight trains, if the slow freight train did not have enough running time to get to Rotherham Road goods loop. If the loop was already full, the train was then put up the bank. A running time of seven minutes for a Class 8 freight train to Aldwalke was required, so train regulation was of prime importance. When a freight train was shunted up the bank it was not a popular move with the train crew. It was not so much the going up the bank, but the necessity to reverse a full load back down and over the junction and, in the dark, or in bad weather, this was not an easy task.

With a long block section on the 'down' line, not many slow freight trains had a straight run through but, when traffic was heavy, I could allow a train to proceed to the starter signal well in advance of the junction, reverse the points to the branch line if it was clear, and accept another train. I could do this as I still had the quarter of a mile clearance beyond the home signal.

I had the normal week on each turn of duty for training and then I was placed in charge, after passing the rules. Between the hours of 8 a.m. and 4 p.m. I often had the company of either the yard shunter or the numbertaker and, if I was on twelve hours duty, from 6 a.m. to 6 p.m., one of them would kindly go to the local colliery canteen for me and return with a cooked meal. This was a pleasant change from eating sandwiches all the time. Food could be a problem in any signal box, and if your relief did not arrive after your eight hours duty were up, you had to stop for another four hours extra duty, or until a relief signalman could be found. Fortunately, this did not happen very often.

Most signalmen kept, in their locker, some emergency food, mostly tinned so it would keep, and when required it was used and quickly replaced, as you never knew when you might have to work overtime. On the morning and afternoon turns of duty, when the branch line was open, the local trip train crews would come to the signal box for their food and a talk and, in exchange, we never went short of coal for the signal box fire.

The night turn of duty was very lonely, and on most nights I did not see anyone at all because, apart from the time of night, the signal box was a good ten minutes walk from the village and, apart from a small farm, there was nothing nearby except fields and a colliery waste tip. In the summer it was very pleasant, but in the winter it was bleak and isolated.

At the rear of the signal box ran the River Don and the canal, so Thrybergh Junction had a location that was prone to foggy weather. Many times I have seen the sun shining down the valley but, at the same time, I have had fog and the fogman on duty. The line from Thrybergh Junction to Aldwalke ran, for most of the way, parallel to the old LMS line, and my 'up' distant signal was at the rear of Roundwood signal box on the other railway. Therefore, after the fog had cleared, and I required the fogman to come off duty, I used the local sidings telephone to ring the box where the LMS signalman would kindly pass a message to the LNER fogman, and there cannot be many places where that was carried out.

It was a peaceful and friendly railway, typical of the old GCR routes where nobody rushed about. The local trip trains had been known to stop in section to feed the swans on the colliery tip ponds, as the trains pottered around from siding to siding, but so long as the local collieries were well-served, and no passenger trains or fast freight trains were delayed, nobody seemed to mind, and if a signalman required a lift home, he just stopped a light engine for a ride. If a train crew wanted an early finish they would receive a good run over branch line; so it worked both ways.

Summer was over, and I faced my first winter in charge of a signal box. I was not looking forward to the 5 a.m. start on a Monday morning as the box, after being closed since 5 a.m. Sunday, would be very cold and with no fire lit, it was not a very cheerful start to the week. To rise at 4 a.m. was bad enough at the best of times, but on a winter's morning, with frost on the inside of the box windows, it was not much fun. Early starts are part of a signalman's way of life, but with three regular shifts it was much better than the train crews' hours, as they started and finished any time within the twenty four hours. Their starting time could be altered, and the time they finished would depend on the weather, the amount of train delay or just the wait for a ride back to their home depot and, because my father was a guard, I knew from first hand experience the problems this caused to both home and social life.

One afternoon, Control rang to tell me that there had been a derailment on the GNR main line between Retford and Doncaster, and that some main line passenger trains would be diverted via Sheffield. As a result, extra care would have to be taken with train regulations. The circuit telephone message confirmed the diversions, with news of a King's Cross to Newcastle express passenger train passing Darnall near Sheffield. After the local passenger trains this one was something special and it was a joy to watch as it passed; a strange but welcome visitor to the backwater of the railways. After the brief excitement, it turned my thoughts to the GNR main line, instead of slow dirty freight trains to signal. I thought 'why not the top crack express passenger trains, if I could adjust to the high speed traffic'.

February came, and on the vacancy list there was a post that appealed to me, a Class 1 signal box position at New Barnet South, just north of King's Cross. My experience was still limited, but as there were no other jobs on the main line nearer to home, I felt I had to try for the position, and as it was a deferred position it could be months before I moved, even if I was selected.

I received a letter to attend an interview at Great Northern House at King's Cross on Wednesday, 28th February 1962. The other two signalmen were asked to work a duty of twelve hours to cover my time off, and with overtime working the shifts overlapped, so my secret was out. My mates could not understand why I wanted to move and leave home, but I wanted promotion, something that would take years if I stayed where I was, and this was the quickest way. I was successful at the interview, but I was informed it would be towards the end of the year before I had to move to London.

It is strange talking to a signalman over the telephone for hours on end, week after week, and yet never meeting, so we all decided that, as summer was approaching, we would rectify this situation. After the night shift was over, instead of going home to bed, we all met for a swimming session in Rotherham Baths so that friendly voices could now be given a face to match. Further meetings took place on Sunday nights in a pub, so the circuit telephone calls now had a more personal touch to the conversations.

In August, the signalmen's working hours were reduced which meant, in turn, vacancies for rest day relief signalmen to cover the extra hours. I was a Class 1 signalman in name only, and still waiting to move to London, but I could still apply for the next move up to a special class. The signal boxes that I had wanted to work in at Mexborough were Class 1 so a move would rule them out for a regular job, but it was a golden opportunity and one I was not going to miss.

The rest day jobs only covered two shifts, days and afternoons, and with no night or weekend work the money was basic only but, as a single man, it would be enough and I would gain far more time for a social life.

I applied for all the vacancies within a fifty mile radius of home with preference given to the GNR main line and I was lucky for I received notification of an interview for a position at Retford. I spent hours studying the rules and regulations because I knew the interview would be tough because of my tender years, and because the position was so important. I wondered if I could accept the responsibility and the hard work.

I passed the interview but I could not really believe it because, after only eighteen months as a signalman, I had moved from a Class 3 to a special class. It also meant that I would not be going to London, but only as far as Retford, some 25 miles away. I had a few easy weeks left before the big move.

One very foggy November night, I took over duty at 9.40 p.m. This was a little early, but it would give my mate a chance to travel home just in case the buses stopped running and, in the few minutes we spent talking, I was given the latest information. All the signals were off on the 'down' main line for a Class 7 freight train from Mexborough to Annesley; the same train that had caused problems for me as a shunter. Also, the 'is line clear' bell signal had been received for the 'up' main line for a Sheffield to Doncaster passenger train. In addition, he informed me that the branch line was closed and the fogmen had been sent for but were not yet on duty, and I was told the number of wagons in the sidings plus other information which signalmen passed to one another when changing duty.

I filled my pipe and prepared for a hard night's work as Kilnhurst gave me the 'train on line' signal for the 'down' freight. Then, just as I was about to sit down, I received the 'train on line' signal from Aldwalke for the 'up' passenger train. I moved to the Kilnhurst bell to forward the train when the signalman there rang me. This was strange, but I answered immediately, and received the emergency signal of 7 bells 'stop and examine train'. The guard had shown a red light passing the box at Kilnhurst, and that was all I knew.

Now I had a problem. The passenger train was approaching on the 'up' line, and it had to be stopped. The 'up' signals were at 'danger', but in thick fog, without a fogman on duty, they could easily be missed, adding to the fact that I had a very bad home signal which was hard to spot, because of its height. In addition, on the opposite line, there was a train which I also had to stop, as something was wrong.

I very quickly replaced all the 'down' signals back to 'danger', but I knew the driver would have seen and passed the distant signal in the 'clear' position, which gave him a clear run almost to Rotherham. I checked the paraffin hand lamp, which was always lit after dark and in bad weather, but with its poor light, the fog and the steam from the engine the driver would be very lucky to see it. Both sets of emergency detonators were placed on both lines, but would the trains stop before disaster struck? The rules had been carried out and there was little else I could do. Then my past training automatically came back to me from my duties as a shunter; use my whistle. Signal boxes are not issued with whistles but I had kept mine in my locker, and if the driver did not see the red hand signal I felt sure the shrill of the whistle would carry to him over the noise of the engine. I rushed to the end window and opened it, to hear the freight train engine at full steam climbing up the hill with a full and heavy load. It was still moving fast so the driver had seen the distant signal which was off, so he was still unaware of the tense situation and the danger. Then, with a great roar, the engine appeared out of the fog so I waved the red lamp and blew the whistle as hard as I could.

There was the sudden but welcome sound of the engines brakes going hard on meaning that the driver had either seen the lamp or heard the whistle. Then the 'down' set of detonators were exploding as the train lost speed, before stopping half-way across the junction.

The driver had done very well to stop as quickly as he did but I only had one train stopped and, because the brake van was still some distance

46

away, I still did not know what the trouble was and on the 'up' line, the passenger train was still coming towards us.

Suddenly, everything happened at once. The freight train driver came running back as his guard came rushing forward, but the best sound of all was the engine whistle of the 'up' passenger train protesting at being stood at the home signal. All the immediate danger was now over, but I had to find out what exactly was happening. The freight train driver arrived at the box first and, roughly translated, he said, 'The distant signal was off so why have you stopped my train?'. His guard then arrived on the scene and answered the question, and it turned out that something was wrong with one of the wagons. Both men were then sent off back down the train, to ascertain precisely what the trouble was.

A light then shone through the fog as the fireman of the 'up' passenger train walked to the signal box to carry out Rule 55. This rule stated that when a train had been brought to a stand, owing to a stop signal being at 'danger', the fireman had to go to the signal box and remind the signalman of the position of his train. He wrote in the train register book, Rule 55 for his train, and then signed his name against the entry together with the time, and I initialled it. On his way up he had passed the freight train stood across the junction and he enquired what the trouble was, so I told him all I knew, which was very little. I also told him how pleased I was that his train had stopped, and then he returned back to report to his driver before going to offer his assistance to the freight crew.

The mystery was solved when the train crews came back to the signal box to explain what had happened. The guard had heard an unusual loud banging noise but in the darkness and fog was unable to see what the problem was, but he knew something was wrong. A sliding door on a fitted parcels van had come away from its fastening, and the banging was the door moving about. Luck was on our side because the van was empty, but if it had been loaded its goods would have fallen out all over the track, possibly blocking the opposite line and even causing a derailment or damage to other trains. The guard had rightly put safety first, and that was why all trains have to be stopped.

The train crews had fixed the door and they gave me all the details for Control including the wagon number and its destination, so everything was now back to normal. Thanks to the common sense and the experience of all concerned, what could have been a major accident turned out to be just a fright.

I reported all the details to Control after which both trains then departed and, after replacing the used detonators, I wrote out my report giving reasons for the delay. After clearing the backlog of trains held up I then sat down for a welcome cup of tea and a pipe of tobacco, thankful that everything had turned out all right in the end.

November had passed, and the new rest day relief duties were slowly being filled, so I knew I would soon be on my way to Retford and the GNR main line, but not before I had another experience; a runaway train.

It all happened on the branch line, around mid-morning, on a very cold and wet December day. The gradient was all downhill from Silverwood to Thrybergh and it was the practice for all freight trains from Silverwood Colliery to stop at the next signal box, Don Bridge, so that the guard could pick up the wagon brakes before the train continued down the hill to join the main line at Thrybergh Junction.

The facing points at Don Bridge were always set to a position so that if a train was running away, it could safely run down an old line to stop some miles away on level track in an old siding. In this instance, the coal freight train had stopped at the home signal, so the signalwomen rightly reversed the points towards the main line, and the train moved slowly forward towards the starting signal which was at 'danger'.

This move happened with every train because the special instructions at Thrybergh were that before acceptance from Don Bridge, the junction points must be set to the main line with the home signal in the off position, and we only accepted the trains when they were ready because the junction could not be blocked for long.

That particular morning the platelayers were working on the track on the branch line, at its junction with the main line. They had a look-out man on duty but, as an extra precaution, I also shouted to them when a train was approaching. They had asked me for a few minutes without a train passing so they could jack up and pack a section of track and, as the line was quiet, I gave permission. I had been offered the 'is line clear' signal for the trip freight train but it was not accepted because the train was not ready, and the track was not clear.

The platelayers could see the train and they told me the track was nearly finished when, to our horror, the engine started slipping on the wet rails. This was due to the weight of the loaded coal wagons and the downhill gradient combining to slowly push the train past the starting signal which was set at 'danger'.

There was a set of trap points to protect the main line but the problem was that a train coming off the track would crash into the end of the signal box, as had happened years before necessitating the rebuilding of the box. The train would finish up in the river or, if the points were set for the main line and if the train was running fast, it would become derailed, and block all the lines.

After receiving the bell signal 4+5+5 'train or vehicles running away in right direction', I now had to decide which course of action to take. I could now clearly see the train and hear the popping of the engine's whistle as the driver fought to regain control, but without any success. The platelayers moved very quickly to remove the jacks while casting an eye towards the runaway train, and I could only watch and wait to see which one would win the race against time.

The ganger then shouted that the track was clear and I could see the train was still moving, slower now, but still out of control, so I set the junction points to main line, pulled off the signals to help the driver, and stood back to watch as the train came off the junction at a speed slower than normal. The right team had won the race against time.

The freight train was shunted into the yard sidings, and the train crew came in to the signal box along with the platelayers. It looked like I would have to act as a peacemaker if a row broke out.

What had happened was that the guard had picked up the wagon brakes too early, when the train had stopped at Don Bridge home signal, instead of waiting until it had reached the starting signal and, because of

Kilnhurst signal box, photographed in 1966.

The view from Kilnhurst box looking towards Rotherham.

From the same location, but this time looking towards Mexborough and Doncaster.

The author, standing just to the right of the lady, pictured with some
workmates before going swimming.

Thrybergh Junction 1962. The morning Worksop Bullcroft freight coming off the branch line.

Thrybergh Junction signal box, as it was in 1962.

Wath upon Dearne yard, showing part of the telex office (bottom-right).

Wath upon Dearne signal box, on the old LMS line, with No. 4472 *Flying Scotsman* passing on a special train.

A York to Bournemouth Express passing Kilnhurst box in 1961.

Mexborough Station.

Thrybergh Colliery box, photographed *circa* 1890. It was later replaced
by Thrybergh Junction box around 1905.

Thrybergh Junction box *circa* 1905, built after the opening of the Silverwood branch.

A runaway train from the Silverwood branch, pictured at the run-off traps at Thrybergh Junction around 1906.

the wet rails, the steam engine could not hold the train. The train crew were happy that they did not have to jump out of the moving train or have a December bath in the river, and leave the train swimming with the fish. The guard was a new man and, because it was all his fault, he was rather shaken, but after a cup of tea, he was all right.

The platelayers were happy because the track had not been damaged and, as no one was hurt, everything was now all right. I had to report the incident because the bell signals had been recorded, but a few days later I spoke with the guard who had received a written warning about his actions, so the whole incident was now closed.

I received my transfer to Retford in January, so I bid farewell to Thrybergh Junction, the old Great Central Railway and all my mates, and set off to a different railway and a new way of life.

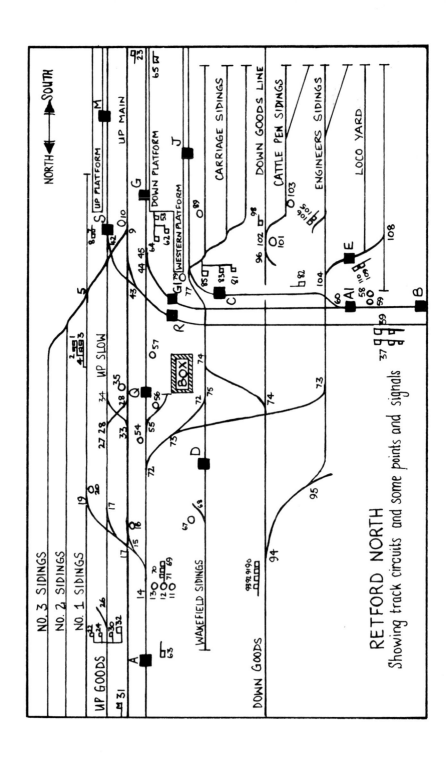

RETFORD NORTH
Showing track circuits and some points and signals

# Chapter Seven
# The Main Line

I set off for Retford feeling like a little boy lost, in railway terms a country boy making his first visit to a large city. The train departed and I stood on the 'up' platform to take a brief look around, before taking the first step in a new environment. The stationmaster's office was my first objective where I was shown the plan of the station and told where to send my time-sheets and where to collect my wages. I was then directed to the District Signalling Inspector's office, on the 'down' side platform.

The 'down' main line signals were all off and I was just about to cross the lines when suddenly, from around the curve at Retford South, an express passenger train came towards me at full speed and, in a split second, the 'Deltic' had flashed past me, leaving an air vacuum in its wake. I then decided that the only way to cross was via the subway which I should have done at first, but it served to teach me my first lesson about the speed of the trains on the King's Cross to Edinburgh main lines.

It was a very long interview with the District Inspector in which every rule and signalling regulation came under discussion because, at my age, he had to know if I knew them all. I was told about the area, the three signal boxes I would cover, and other interesting facts. Then, as I seemed satisfactory, I was told to report for duty and to start my training at Grove Road signal box in the morning.

I was over the first hurdle in my ambition to become a signalman on the main line. It had been a long and hard day, but tomorrow I would return back to the signal box to start a new career on a line that was new to me.

I decided to walk down the line, remembering yesterday's fright, but it was the only way to see the local signals, level crossings, and to find out about the area. I had seen Retford North and Thrumpton Crossing, my other two boxes, from the station and after my mile walk I came to my third box, Grove Road.

What a surprise. I did not know what to expect, but I found a very small signal box, even smaller than my first box at Kilnhurst; not what I imagined at all as I thought all the signal boxes would be rather large and grand.

I went up the steps and entered the box, to find an elderly signalman on duty. He looked at me and asked if I was the new rest day relief man and after I had replied that I was, I was told in no uncertain terms that I was far too young for the job, and also a stranger to the line.

What a welcome! After the help I had received from the signalmen on the GCR I found his actions a little strange. I thought he might be jealous of my classification but that could not be the reason because, with over 45 years experience behind him, the position would have been his if he had wanted it. I sat down on the locker to accustom myself with the box and then lit up my pipe, but this action was followed by the sudden opening of all the windows with not a word being said. Thus I put the pipe away, instead of freezing on this cold January morning.

A bell rang so I got up to answer it, but was beaten to it by a suddenly spritely old man. After a while I was told that if I had to learn the box I first had to look after the gates, which meant turning a big heavy wheel which opened or closed the level crossing gates in readiness for every train to pass. After half an hour I had practised enough so I insisted that I now used the bells and levers and, with a great deal of reluctance, this was allowed although I was critically watched all the time.

At 2 p.m., the signalman changed over, and the afternoon man made me feel at home and very welcome. He explained that the day signalman acted the same with everybody, and I had to remember two things about him when I was in charge. One, to relieve him on time and two, if he relieved me, I had to make sure the signal box was left very neat and clean. My hours for training were flexible, so I decided I would work on the afternon turn of duty to save any ill feeling.

Grove Road was a Class 1 signal box with only twenty levers, two main lines, an 'up' goods loop, an 'up' siding and a crossover road, the latter two items looking as if they had never been used. Apart from the gates, Grove Road was only a block post with traffic regulation on the 'up' lines, and a lot more faster trains.

Steam had virtually disappeared by now, and the express passenger trains were now hauled by Class 55 'Deltic' or Class 47 Brush diesels. As they passed the signal box at 70 to 80 m.p.h., I had to learn to be quick at getting the level crossing gates shut and all the signals off for at that speed, there was little margin for error.

Train regulation on the 'up' line was very critical because a Class 7 freight train running main line, with an uphill gradient most of the way to the next goods loop at Dukeries Junction, required a running time of at least twenty minutes to avoid stopping a following passenger train. To assist with train regulation, the express trains were reported passing either Selby or Wakefield, both locations being about 37 miles away, and this was done by the block telegraph single needle, a morse code method used instead of the circuit telephones, because of the number of boxes and the distance involved. I had spent some time at Doncaster Signalling School to learn the telegraph but I was never happy with it because if it was sent quickly, I would invariably have difficulty reading it. Fortunately, if I missed a message, my mate at the next box up the line, who also received the same message, would kindly pass on the information to me.

The 'down' trains were not a problem at Grove Road as they just ran block to block, simply following one another. Absolute Block working was used between Grove Road and Retford South and, in the other direction, Absolute Block was used between Grove Road and Gamston, on the main lines, with Goods Permissive used on the 'up' goods loop. The freight trains were reported into the Control office when they entered the loop and that was all that was reported, except anything out of the ordinary.

After only a few days training, I moved to my second signal box, Thrumpton Crossing. This was a Special Class A box and it was on the old GCR line between Cleethorpes and Grimsby, to and from Worksop and Sheffield, and I was back on familiar type workings again. Local passenger and slow freight trains were plentiful, but most of the work was with the GCR locomotive shed. Light engines were forever moving, if not on the main lines then inside the loop line, going from the turntable to the shed or to the locomotive sidings.

Absolute Block was used on the 'up' and 'down' main lines to Retford South, with Permissive Freight on the 'down' goods. When Retford South required to occupy the 'up' main line for a train drawing forward for shunting, a special bell code of 3+4+1 was used and withdrawn with 8 bells. In the other direction to Gringley Road, the Absolute Block was used. Two sets of level crossing gates were used with one set always shut every time an engine was moved on or off the shed, so there was plenty of hard manual work. Retford South, with its famous straight crossing, was only 431 yds. away, so the main thing to keep an eye on was the keeping of trains moving and clear of the main line.

After a month, I moved to my third signal box and the biggest challenge of all, Special Class B Retford North, and what a box it was to work. It had everything and I had never seen a box so large or so busy. My first reaction was almost one of fright as I thought I would never learn to work it and, in fact, it took me nearly two months hard training before I could do so.

Falling under the box's jurisdiction were the GNR main line, the junction to and from Sheffield, station platforms, station pilots, 'up' sidings, 'up' goods, 'up' platform lines, 'down' slow, 'down' goods, passenger carriage sidings, cattle sidings, engineer's sidings and engine sheds. Lines and points were everywhere, including 'up' main to 'up' platform, 'up' goods to 'up' yard, Sheffield Junction to main line or platform and engine shed to carriage sidings; to name but a few.

There was Absolute Block, Permissive Block, Platform Permissive, a whole shelf of block bells, 22 block indicators and over 120 levers. Trains were passing on all lines, with through passenger trains travelling at over 75 m.p.h.

With the close proximity of the other boxes, Retford South, with its five lines, was only 390 yds. away and every time a wheel turned at Retford Station, a train or engine had to be signalled and levers moved. There was a train register boy on each shift, and both the signalman and his train register boy were lucky if they could find enough free time to have a cup of tea or a sandwich, for it was a very tiring box to work, both physically and mentally.

I knew about train regulation with freight trains, but now I had to do it with passenger trains as well, because some of the main line passenger trains that stopped at Retford were a booked connection with the local services. If all the trains were running to time, it was hard enough, but you only required one late train and it was problem time. One mistake, or a wrong train on a wrong line, or bad timing, could cause havoc, and it could take hours before the system was again running smoothly.

At the ripe old age of 22, and with two years experience, this was what I had to face but, with the confidence of youth combined with strength and energy, I managed but, on reflection, I often wondered how. I worked very well with the train register boys because they were of my own age group, so we spoke the same language, of girls, football and records. The signalmen at Retford North had a great deal of understanding while I was training and, when the traffic was extra busy, they were glad of an extra pair of hands.

With two shift workings in winter I was now finding the travelling tough, as, to arrive at Retford North for 6 a.m. I had to rise by 4.30 a.m., to leave home by 5 a.m., then ride 25 miles on a motor cycle across lonely country roads, have a hard shift, then face the cold ride back again. On the 2 p.m. turn, I could travel out by a passenger train, but the return journey was sometimes awkward. If my train was late, I missed my connection at Doncaster for Mexborough, meaning that I had to rush across town to catch the last bus to Conisbrough then walk the last three miles home. In the summer, the motor cycle would solve this problem.

One evening, I had a ride home, and it was a trip I will always remember. A light engine from Grantham to Rotherham, running via Doncaster and Mexborough for a return working, arrived just in front of my passenger train as I climbed aboard a Class A3 Pacific. We then set off and I was given the fireman's seat, as he was busy keeping the fire going. I marvelled at the skill of the enginemen and especially the driver who was aware he was in front of the passenger train and, as we roared through the dark winter's night, how he found the signals and read them I did not know. With the fireman still bent over, working with his shovel, I suddenly realized what a hard rough job they had, and how much they depended on the signalman.

I arrived home early, but I knew I was going to have to move and live in Retford. Then, quite out of the blue, a railwayman helped me out. Grove Road was the only box out of the three I worked where I had time to spend on the circuit telephone and, talking one day to a relief signalman about moving, he told me his parents had a spare room so the following weekend I moved in with them. Coming from a railway family I found myself with another, and it was a great help because they understood all about signal boxes, shift work and a railwayman's way of life.

At the end of April I was in charge, so I settled down to enjoy the work and the new company. In South Yorkshire, when a man is off work, he was 'laiking' and, as I used this expression in my rough Yorkshire accent to Nottinghamshire men one day, they found me hard to understand, but it helped to break the ice, and I was accepted.

Every signalman, if he is truthful, will at sometime or another make a mistake in train regulation and, as a new man, I was careful about this, but one Saturday morning at Grove Road I made a mistake. I had received the 'train on line' signal from Retford South for an 'up' Class 8 freight train and, knowing it required twenty minutes to run to Dukeries Junction, I put the train into the goods loop to clear the morning Sheffield to London (King's Cross) Pullman train. After the freight train had passed, and was en route towards Gamston signal box, my mate there came on to the block telephone to enquire why the freight train was in the loop line, so I said that it was because the Pullman express was due.

He told me that the freight train crew would be rather upset waiting until Monday morning, because the Pullman did not run on Saturdays or Sundays. I had a list pinned up in the box with the passing times of all the passenger trains on it, but I had missed the 'Saturday excepted' note. After the other lads had stopped laughing at my mistake the freight train was let out of the loop to proceed, the driver, no doubt, wondering what the signalman was doing. It is a pity, after such a mistake, that a signalman cannot apologize to a driver.

On another Saturday morning, again at Grove Road signal box but in the summer, I took a gamble on train regulation. The day before I had been working Retford North box and the driver of an 'up' freight train, while waiting to shunt in the yard sidings, called into the box to ask me to try to give him a good run tomorrow, as he wanted to be back at Doncaster early to catch a train to go on his holidays, and gain an extra day. I explained I was at Grove Road, and I would try to do my best for him.

When his train was signalled it was well short of running time and, with a London express passenger train already past Doncaster behind him, the freight train should have gone into the goods loop, so I wondered what to do. If the driver had decided to stop at home I would be in trouble for stopping the express but, if he was working the train, and I had the nerve to give him a run, I would help him.

I telephoned back down the line to enquire how the train was running, and was told it was going fast. After forwarding the 'is line clear' signal to Gamston Main Line box, my mate there reminded me of the express and the consequences if I should stop it, but I took full responsibility, shut the gates, and gave him the back board, as the distant signal is sometimes known, 'right away'.

I have never seen a freight train going so fast as, with a friendly wave, the driver passed me running at almost passenger speed. I was now on tenterhooks hoping he would clear the express but true to his word he did, with time to spare. The same engineman was wired on for the return journey of 'light engine home', and again he passed me going like the proverbial bomb. I would never know if he caught his train, but at least I had done my best to help him.

Anything out of the ordinary always happened to me on the day shift at Grove Road box and this time, it was a November day. I received the 'is line clear' bell signal from Retford South and 4 bells for the 1E04, the 7.50 a.m. Leeds to King's Cross passenger train, due to depart from Retford Station at 9.10 a.m. I closed the level crossing gates to the road traffic only to find the gate stopper would not come up to lock the gates which, in turn, apart from the danger of a swinging gate, locked the home signal. Thus I had a crossing gate failure and another problem.

The signal & telegraph men dealt with signal or points failure so I quickly telephoned them for assistance, only to find they were working on another failure to the north of Retford. If they left there immediately it would be at least twenty minutes before they reached me, and then they had to solve the problem. I tried the gates again and again with the same result, and it looked as if the express was going to be delayed, with a great deal of inconvenience for the many businessmen aboard with appointments in the City, but there was nothing else I could do.

I went outside to check the gate locks but could not find anything wrong and I was running out of time. An idea then came to me so I dashed into the bottom room for some rope to tie the gates in position, but could only find one small length. Fortunately it was long enough to do one gate, so I made fast the gate which was furthest from the train.

Returning back to the box I passed the train bell signal forward, pulled No. 8 lever for the 'up' main starter signal, which was not locked by the gate failure, and grabbed the green flag off the wall to return outside and solve the problem.

The express train had nearly stopped, the driver sounding the whistle for the signals to clear, so I held the gate closed with one hand and stood in front of it and, with my other hand, held up the green flag. The driver acknowledged my signal and proceeded very slowly past the home signal at 'danger' until he could clearly see what had happened then, seeing the starter signal off, he accelerated away.

I was now holding the gate closed with both hands and the engine and the coaches were now passing very close to me but I held on and, after what seemed a lifetime, they were clear. I returned back to the box to report the delay to Control and after the signal & telegraph men had repaired the fault and the line was back to normal, I was left with aching arms but with the satisfaction of a job done well.

By now, steam engines were nearly a thing of the past but one day, at Retford North, I had the pleasure to signal and then see an old favourite, a Class A4 Pacific. It was not working a passenger train but a fully-fitted cement train from Uddingston Cliffe, instead of the normal pair of Southern Region Class 33 diesels. When she passed up the main line with all signals off she was a splendid sight, even if the old engine was maybe past her best.

After a very happy year at Retford, a vacancy arose for a similar position at Doncaster, and I reluctantly decided once again to move. I was sorry to leave Retford, for I had enjoyed my stay. I had played football for a local team, met some good railwaymen, stopped with a grand old couple who treated me like a son and not a lodger, and I had gained some experience with working three signal boxes.

Doncaster was only eight miles from my home and within easy travelling, distance, and now a few of my old mates from the Great Central Railway were working in Doncaster and I looked forward to meeting them again. I was ready to accept another challenge.

# Chapter Eight
# Doncaster

Doncaster is exactly 156 miles from London (King's Cross) and 112 miles from Newcastle, and the first railway came here in the 1840s. This was the Great Northern Railway's main line, which roughly followed the route of the old Great North Road (A1) from London to Edinburgh. Doncaster is well-known for its locomotive and carriage works, commonly referred to as The Plant.

It was here where some of the world's best-known steam engines were built including the world record holder for the fastest steam engine, Sir Nigel Gresley's Class A4 Pacific *Mallard*, and the equally legendary Class A3, *Flying Scotsman*.

My first signal box was about three miles south from The Plant and the station and was the Class 1 Black Carr Junction box. It was an interesting box but rather straightforward, its main feature being the junction to and from Gainsborough and Lincoln. It also had main and goods lines but no sidings and no level crossing gates, but with both Absolute and Permissive Block signalling, and with only fifty levers to work, plus a train register boy to assist, I found it an easy box to operate.

My next workplace was Red Bank signal box, (Special Class A) which was situated at the south end of Doncaster locomotive shed, with three running lines on the 'down' side, the 'up' main line and 'up' sidings. A large amount of the work was done in conjunction with the nearby Carr Box, with a special code of bells and interlocking points and signals for the light engines to Carr Shed, resulting in a lot of hard work and, with 100 levers in the frame, it was a busy box but not one of great interest.

There was a document from the past kept in Red Bank box which proved the old signalman there had led a hard working life. It listed the number of trains dealt with for four weeks in 1931.

| | |
|---|---|
| Week Commencing Monday 9th February 1931 | 1,956 |
| Week Commencing Monday 13th April 1931 | 1,907 |
| Week Commencing Monday 10th August 1931 | 2,109 |
| Week Commencing Monday 12th October 1931 | 1,866 |
| *Total for 4 Weeks* | 7,838 |

This made the daily average of trains 326.5 and, in 24 hours, the levers were pulled, pushed or replaced 4,252 times, 1,417 per man, per shift. With telephones to answer, records to keep and shift working, these men certainly deserved their money. I do not know what this year's figure would be to compare, but it certainly is not as high.

My third signal box was something special, Doncaster South (Special Class A), just off the end of Doncaster Station. It was an all power box and, instead of levers there were small switches and instead of block bells and indicators there were train describers, which gave a visual illuminated panel. It was more like working in an office than a signal box and it was manned by two signalmen, one to work the 'up' trains the other to work the 'down' trains, working one week on one side and the following week the other. A train recording boy made up the team.

There were all types of signal rules and special instructions, with Permissive working being used for passenger trains. Therefore it was a very busy box, and we worked closely with its sister type at the other end of the station, Doncaster North.

I found the South box had one big advantage over my other boxes because, with two signalmen on duty, when there was a quiet spell, one man would cover both jobs so that the other could have a meal, and then it worked vice versa. Also, you had time to visit the toilet while your mate covered your duties; handy after a night out.

Traffic was heavy, of course, even in the winter months, and on the 'down' side only for the winter season 1963/4, here are some examples taken from the station list which, of course, applied to the passenger trains only.

| Number | Time | Train | From | In | Platform | Out | Destination |
|---|---|---|---|---|---|---|---|
| 1A36 | 2.20 | King's Cross | | 5.18 | 8 | 5.24 | York |
| 2N57 | ECS | Ex-Garden Sidings | | | 5 | 5.30 | Leeds |
| 1A42 | 3.00 | King's Cross | | 5.39 | 5 | 5.42 | Newcastle |
| 2L38 | 5.08 | Sheffield | | 5.47 | 8 | 5.55 | Cleethorpes |
| 1N21 | 3.20 | King's Cross | | 5.55 | 5 | 5.58 | Leeds |
| 1N31 | 4.10 | Manchester | | 6.01 | 8 | 6.10 | Hull |
| 1A46 | 4.00 | King's Cross | | pass at 6.17 p.m. | | | Edinburgh |

This was part of the afternoon shift, and with the 'up' working being very similar with the addition of all the empty coaching stock, freight trains both fast and slow and light engines, things could be very hectic. This only included the normal trains and did not include any special passenger trains, for which a path had to be found, or extra freight, and this was only the winter season, and it got busier in the summer.

I enjoyed working the 'up' panel the most as I was dealing with trains leaving the platforms, not just running in as on the 'down' side and, with trains to Sheffield crossing all the junctions, I had to be careful about regulations. The timetables and platform lists were essential to ensure the right train went into the right platform, but some of the information did not do justice to the trains. For example, 1A35, 10.00 Edinburgh London pass 13.37 was all the information given for the famous 'up' 'Flying Scotsman' or on the 'down' side, it read 1S57, 12.00 King's Cross Glasgow pass 14.31 for the 'Queen of Scots' Pullman train.

I had shunted freight trains before, but here at Doncaster I was now shunting passenger trains because of the special working at a large passenger station. One very good example was the 'up' morning (1E28) 10.10 'Yorkshire Pullman' from Hull, which joined up with the (1E08) 09.52 service from Harrogate to go forward to London (King's Cross).

The Hull portion would arrive in platform 1 at 11.08 where the engine came off to depart for a return working, the Harrogate portion then arriving in platform 4. The engine would uncouple then move on to platform 1 and attach the Hull train, which was then moved to the 'up' slow passenger line and reversed back to platform 4 to join up, before departing at 11.22 as the 1E08 non-stop service to London. This manoeuvre was worked from Mondays to Fridays, but it could be tricky if one or other of the trains arrived late. The train also split up on the return journey in the evening.

One of the most interesting passenger trains was the (1V67) 18.40 York to Swindon service which arrived at 19.32, was shunted in the platform bays to collect more parcel vans, then left at 19.50 to call at Mexborough, Rotherham (Central), Sheffield (Victoria), Nottingham, Loughborough, Leicester, Rugby, Banbury, Oxford and Swindon. This was one of the great cross-country trains, one of the few left.

With four regular signalmen working North and South boxes, it was very different on the few occasions when four relief and rest day men were on duty at the same time. The reason for this was simple because, apart from me, the other three men knew both boxes and with the close proximity of the two boxes, they all knew what the men at the other end of the station were doing, and why. Trains that would normally have waited to go via the slow line were kept running via the fast lines and goods trains ran through the platform lines, but the station bottleneck was reduced, and the traffic flowed.

Due to the lack of physical work in the South box, I overcame this by playing football for the Doncaster branch of the British Rail Staff Association, and cricket with the Swinton branch. I entered some railway competitions but without success and my rest days would be spent travelling all over the railway network, so my life was totally centred around the railway.

One of the problems with railway life was the shift working, particularly if you lived some distance away from your duties but, with a car and a good train and bus service, I had little trouble but, as every car driver knows, they always break down at the wrong time. It happened to me at 11 p.m. on a bank holiday Sunday night when I needed the car for 5 a.m. the following morning, for duty at Black Carr Junction. After failing to book a taxi, I decided I could catch the 04.20 Sheffield to Leeds train at 04.45, from Mexborough to Doncaster, then either walk the three miles to the box or, if I was lucky, get a taxi from the station, with no buses running at that hour on a bank holiday.

The train was late so I arrived in Doncaster at 5.30 a.m., too late to walk to the box and, because there were no main line passenger trains due, there were no taxis. I had a problem because at 6 a.m. the box had to close, the signalman on duty having worked his full twelve hour Sunday night turn, returning for duty at 2 p.m. If the box shut then the main line would still be kept open but the junction could not, and a passenger train was due over the junction about 6 a.m., so I dashed back to the South box on the off chance of a lift on a freight train.

Nothing was lit up on the train describer 'up' lines except in platform 4 where the (2J96) 05.55 passenger train to Gainsborough, Saxilby and Lincoln was about to depart, leaving the main line at Black Carr. A passenger train on any railway is important, particularly on a main line, and if he stopped it a signalman would receive a letter from the stationmaster to explain the reasons for the delay. My idea was to use the passenger train for a lift to work.

The train had a tight timing on the main line but, after leaving Black Carr, it had a recovery time on the branch line to Gainsborough, and there was a permanent speed restriction of 15 m.p.h. at Black Carr through the junction to the branch. Therefore, if the train passed through slowly, a railwayman, who had been used to getting off moving trains as a shunter, could alight, and all I had to do now was convince the driver.

I knew it was strictly against the rules to ride on and then stop a passenger train en route but I considered this an emergency and the train was not a fast express, but more of a slow passenger and parcels, so I explained to the driver that if I could not get the ride, his train would come to a stand, with Black Carr box shut. The driver naturally was very much against the idea but, after thinking about the situation, decided that a slight delay would be better than a long stop and after I agreed to take the blame for any delay, he reluctantly agreed to my proposal. I became, therefore, one of the very few signalmen ever to have a lift to work on a passenger train, and to have it stop en route for me.

As we left Doncaster, I was trying to think of a reason to give first Control and then the stationmaster for the train's delay, but the driver came to my rescue saying that if the train was on time reaching Gainsborough and the guard agreed, they would forget to report the slight delay. I thanked the train crew and, as the train slowly passed the junction, I got off and went up the signal box steps to report for duty on time. The train was early reaching Gainsborough, so thanks to the train crew my drastic move had worked, and without anyone knowing.

Unusual occurrences are all part of a signalman's work, and I always maintained that as long as all the rules and regulations were strictly worked to, any real emergency could be overcome.

One morning, I was on duty at Red Bank signal box and the (1N03) 07.45 King's Cross to Leeds train due to reach Doncaster at 10.15, had just passed, and I had accepted from Decoy No. 1 box the (1A06) 08.00 King's Cross to Edinburgh non-stop express, due to pass Doncaster at 10.25 but after the normal running time of about a minute, I had not received from Balby Junction the 'train out of section' bell signal for the previous train. I knew the following express would soon have to slow down with the distant signals against it, as my mate at Balby Junction had rung to tell me that all lines were stopped. An 'up' passenger train had left Doncaster Station with a door open, and it was now stood at Bridge Junction until the lines had been searched to make sure a passenger had not fallen out and was lying injured on the track.

The 'Deltic' stopped at my home signal smoothly and easily, its whistle wailing in protest at the misjustice of stopping such a fine beast in full flight, and the secondman came swiftly to the signal box and enquired, almost demanding to know why the non-stop express passenger train had been stopped. I felt like saying because the signals were at 'danger', but I explained the situation to him and after he had signed the train register book, with a shrug of the shoulders, he returned back to his engine. I reported to Control that the 1A06 stood waiting block, and I also informed the signalman at the box in the rear (Decoy No. 1) of the delay. These incidents were rare, but what I did after was unheard of.

I had a Class 9 freight train with thirty wagons stood on the 'down' transfer line waiting to cross both main lines, to run via the 'down' arrivals line to Belmont Yard. The main line was stood empty, the express was waiting at the home signal, Rule 55 had been carried out and I was not breaking any rules, so I set up the points and pulled off the signal to allow the slow freight train to run across the main lines, straight in front of the standing express train.

The freight train driver must have been surprised but his signal was off, so he moved his train forward and, as he passed the box, I stood at the window smiling, as much as to say 'puzzle that move out'. The yard foreman then came to the box to find out what was happening and he said that he had never seen a move like that before in all his career.

I had worked to rule, the points were all replaced, and the main line was again awaiting normal working. I had moved the freight train because after any delay with a main line stood empty there would be a build-up of trains and, by clearing the goods lines, it would help ease the congestion that would follow. Normal working was soon back in operation and the express train went on its way with, I imagine, a few puzzled passengers on board, as it is not every day they have to wait for a freight train to pass them.

Steam had now almost gone, but one famous engine seemed reluctant to leave its home ground, No. 60103 *Flying Scotsman*, and it was forever moving, either live or dead, to and from The Plant and Carr locomotive shed for repairs and servicing.

It was 2 p.m., and I had just finished duty at Red Bank box ready to travel home by train, as the car was in a garage for a service, when I saw the splendid green engine coming out of Carr Shed en route back to The Plant, so I decided it would be a good opportunity to ride on such a wonderful engine. When an engine is dead it has only a rider on it to work the handbrake, therefore I knew there would be a spare seat, so I climbed aboard and off we set, not in steam but in tow behind some nondescript diesel that did not belong in such fine company, and we travelled down the goods line.

As we swayed and bumped over the rails I could feel the footplate moving and could sense the power the engine had, but I felt sad to think that, only a few years previous, this fine engine would have been on the main line next to us now, hauling a fast express train to the North and Scotland at 70 m.p.h. At least, the engine would still run in the future, and not be sent for scrap like so many of its class. We soon arrived at The Plant so I departed, knowing we would meet again at a future date.

Any career has its surprises and a railway career is no different. One Sunday, I was on duty at Doncaster South box, not as a signalman but as an Acting Inspector, to liaise between the signalman and the signal & telegraph men who were testing the points and signals. After a set of points had been checked and serviced, I asked the Signal & Telegraph Inspector about the length of time that would elapse before the points needed attention again, and his reply shook me.

I can only assume he did not know I was a signalman, for he told me that plans had been made for just a few power signal boxes to work the whole line from Edinburgh to London and, with about ten boxes to cover the whole area, all the other boxes were to close. It would not happen for a few years, but it was a future move.

I felt sick at the thought of this, because I would be one of the first to go because of my short length of service. When a box is closed, the signalman, even if he is Special Class, becomes redundant as he does not drop down the grade with the lower class men going, and I found it rather ironical that a high class position did not guarantee a job. The only advantage with a high grade was that when a vacancy came in a lower grade the higher grade men would get it, and still receive their higher rate of pay for a while. Because of this, I could not see any future in signalling.

The only way I could continue up the ladder would be to leave the operating grade and move to the clerical grade as a clerk, a low grade stationmaster, or a Control Office worker, but I could only apply for the lowest grade; Class 4.

In November 1965, a vacancy was advertised that would solve the problem of my future, Class 4 Assistant Controller, Sheffield DMO, located at Rotherham (Westgate). It was near to home but I would be going back to three shift working again, to a position I knew very little about and, to make matters worse, it was in 'enemy' territory, the old LMS Railway, although now classed as part of the Eastern Region.

I applied for the vacancy, passed the interview and the clerical entrance examination and, just before Christmas 1965, moved to start a new career, once more at the bottom grade, now a member of the salaried staff but with less money.

# Chapter Nine
# Control Office

Where are the trains, I asked myself, as I entered the Control room for the very first time. For here I was, a Trainee Assistant Controller expecting to be near a railway, only to find myself in a large office in the middle of Rotherham with the railway over fifteen minutes walk away, completely out of sight and sound.

The second thing I noticed was how quiet it was, with just a few men speaking into headset telephones, no wagons bumping, no engine whistles and no levers moving. I could have been in any office but here I was at the very hub of the railway, the Control Office, with its rows of desks all facing the same way, built up in three tiers, and I was given a chair at a desk with rows of small lights, feeling just like a new starter on the railway which, in this particular branch of the industry, I was.

Before I could start my own duties I had to be taught how the Control Office worked, so my small part would fit in to the whole organization. The Control Office was manned continuously and had the authority of the Traffic Manager or, in other words, their word was law. The office was staffed by three shifts of eight hours with the usual system of day, night, and afternoon turns of duty and, after training, I would become part of the team.

The Deputy Chief Controller was in overall charge of the shift and his was the final word, and if the need should ever arise he could run any position in the office. Yet here he was, apart from leaving a few telephone calls or to deal with a problem, showing me around and explaining how it all worked.

The object of the Control is efficient train and traffic working which, very briefly, arranged clearance of yard and sidings, efficient use of engines and train crews and, in the event of accident or derailment, it guided the trains back to normal workings.

All the Control Office's work was basically the same all over the railway network, and one surprising fact I learnt was that the very first Control Office was at Rotherham (Masborough), opened in 1908. Where we were now was a couple of miles away from there and was part of the old Westgate Station which closed in October 1952, which explained why we were so far away from the railway.

The front row of the office was filled by six men, three Circuit Controllers and three assistants, one Controller and one assistant working as a team to cover a section of lines and stations.

The section nearest to my desk was No. 3 section, which covered the lines just south of Barnsley to Rotherham and Beighton Junction, which is part way to Chesterfield, and known as the 'Old Road'. This section was of great interest to me because it covered the lines near my home and the junction at Wath Road, the place where I spent so many hours as a lad train-spotting.

The middle section was No. 2 section, which covered the lines from Wincobank Junction, just outside Rotherham, to Sheffield (Midland) Station and to Tapton Junction, just outside Chesterfield.

The end section was No. 1 section, which covered the lines from Horns Bridge, south of Chesterfield, to Beighton Junction, the other half of the 'Old Road'. The 'Old Road' was the main line that the London Midland & Scottish Railway used before the railways went to Sheffield. Each section also covered all the branch lines, sidings, signal boxes and stations within that area.

I was told that the Controller was in charge of a section, and that he knew all the details of the line such as how many wagons would be in a siding, what coaches were in a carriage sidings, and if anything went wrong, such as a signal box closed or an engine failure. Also, it was his responsibility to get the section back to normal working quickly.

The Assistant Controller sat in the next seat, and kept a train graph of the position of every train in the section. This was kept up to date by the information fed to him by the signalmen and Station Inspectors and, with both men plugged into the same circuit, they were in touch with everything that happened on that section.

In front of the men there was a large diagram of the section, with a card on a tee to mark the whereabouts of every freight train. Passenger trains were not shown because of their speed over the section, and instead were marked on the graph.

On the second row of desks sat the Engine Controller and his assistant who, again very briefly, had to work with the Motive Power Depot Inspectors and shed foremen in the entire Rotherham area, to ensure that the right engine was on the right train at the right time. If an engine was missing on the booked diagram, was late, or of the wrong class, it was his job to move the engines around or alter the diagram workings, and keep the trains covered with some motive power. By this time I was getting more and more interested, and I realized how little I knew about the operation of a railway system.

The centre desks in the middle row were manned by the Locomotive Relief Controller and the Guard's Relief Controller. They worked together, along with the Train Crew Inspectors at the relief points, to ensure that trains requiring relief had crews waiting and to avoid train crews' overtime, and to keep the train crews to the booked diagram.

Along with the Engine Controller they reported details to the Section Controllers, and they all told me that if I did my job correctly it would, in turn, assist them. I was now to find out why, as we were now approaching my desk, and a position known simply in the office as the 'wiring on man'.

I was to be the link man between the other adjoining Control Offices, supplying the information on freight trains that would arrive on our area, the following being an example of how it all worked.

I sat in front of an illuminated switchboard, with fifty telephone circuits on it, so that if the Sheffield Control light came on, it was my call sign. The 'wiring on man' there would forward to me the freight train details which were, in order, the train number, as found in the working timetable, the time of the train, where it was from, where it was going, the engine number, the number of wagons, the time on duty for the enginemen, the guard and the train crew's home depot. I had then to condense the information into a train ticket, so it would read 8M38, 10.40, Wath, Toton, 48210, 30-45, 09.50, 10.05, Wath. Sometimes, the starting point and the destination were abbreviated to read, for example, WH and TN, using the first and last letters and also, extra wagon details were sometimes added.

I then took the ticket to the Train Crew Controllers and the Engine Controller who then copied the details but, as this example did not require either train crew relief or engine change, it did not concern them, except for the knowledge of what crew and engine were passing through the area. Quite often, if a train crew or engine were required somewhere, then they arranged things accordingly.

The ticket was now taken to the section control, in this instance No. 3 section, who mounted the ticket on a peg which was then inserted just off his diagram. Thus he knew what train was approaching his section, and, when the signalman reported the train, the ticket was moved on to the diagram board.

As the train passed along his section, the ticket was also moved until it was passed to No. 1 section. When the train was well into No. 1 section, I then passed all the details to my opposite number in the Nottingham Area Control Office.

This method was used for every freight train, so I was always in touch with the adjoining Control of either Sheffield, Manchester, Leeds, York, Nottingham, Derby or Wakefield. I found this job very satisfactory and very educational with my railway geography improving every day, but it was a busy task and, at certain times of the day, it was very hard to keep abreast of all the trains.

I found my new job very different from that in the signal box because now, in a low grade, I found myself given orders instead of me giving them. Also, I now worked in a suit instead of a uniform, and meal breaks were taken at a set time.

The Assistant Controllers, all except one, had their meals together, with all five of us in a small room away from the office, the jobs being covered by the Controller or, in my case, the other assistant, the passenger man who was the other man in the office. I learnt a great deal about Control work just by asking questions and listening to the others talking shop, forgiving the fact they were all LMS men, the old rivalry between railway companies still living on.

Exactly one month after entering the office, the unbelievable happened. A vacancy occurred on another shift for a Class 3 Assistant Controller, the passenger man. I applied, and spent all the time I could spare talking to the man on my shift about the position so, after some quick lessons, I passed the interview, and was appointed to the position of Passenger Assistant Controller at a salary of £825 per annum, to start training on 16th May 1966. I had my promotion and I was on the move again, but this time to another desk only three yards away.

Tickets were not required for passenger trains as they were already marked on the section graphs, but instead, every passenger train was listed on sheets giving booked times on and off the whole area covered by

Rotherham Control. I had to fill in the sheets, and account for any lost time. If a passenger train was three minutes late on to our area, but gained time and left the area on time, my task was easy, but if the train was on time into our area but, say, two minutes late on leaving, I had to find out where the time was lost and why.

I would receive a large percentage of this information from the Section Controllers, but if a train had been over time at a station, I had to ring the Inspector or foreman there for his explanation regarding the delay. The line reports were telephoned to the Line Control at Great Northern House in London, and they informed me of any delay to passenger trains into my area which I then passed on to the Controllers, and all the Station Inspectors and foremen concerned.

The summer season was a busy time for a passenger man, and problems, not applicable to a Section Controller, were passed to me. Every Saturday at Sheffield (Midland) Station was hectic, and one problem came up time after time.

A passenger on a long distance train would leave the train to call into the station buffet for refreshments, and the train would leave without him. It was more often a family man with only the tea money on him with his wife and family, tickets, money and luggage still on the departed train. The Station Inspector would forward the details to me and I, in turn, would report these to the next appropriate Control who then reported to the next station which the train stopped at. The passenger's family were then informed that the stranded man would be following on a certain train, so they either waited for that train or continued the journey. I also received similar messages.

The Passenger Man also had emergencies in passenger trains to deal with, usually involving calling an ambulance for a sick passenger or the police to a drunken passenger, but sometimes, something out of the ordinary could be a problem.

One night, a very large, savage dog broke loose in a forward guard's passenger van, and nobody would risk opening the doors to remove the newspapers and parcels. You could be brave sat a few miles away at a desk, but I had to help the station staff to solve the problem. After consultation with the police, I informed the RSPCA who quickly sent an Inspector to the scene with a tranquilizer gun, who shot the dog and then removed the drugged animal from the train. The station staff could now empty the van.

Another incident involved an old lady who, by mistake, boarded the wrong train, and instead of leaving the train insisted it took her to her destination, miles away in another direction. When she was informed that this was impossible, she promptly locked herself in the toilet. At this stage nobody had informed Control, and when the No. 2 Section Controller asked me why the train was still in Sheffield Station, and late, I had to find out, so I received the details from the Station Inspector, giving me another problem to solve.

I telephoned the Railway Police who went to the train, and a policeman talked the old lady into opening the toilet door, but when she saw the uniform she attacked the burly policeman with her umbrella, before slamming the toilet door shut.

The problem now was the delay to the passenger train. We could either let it depart, complete with an old lady who would finish up miles away from her intended destination, or try another approach.

When a passenger train is held at a station it can cause all manner of problems for other trains waiting to use that platform, so the Deputy Chief Controller was told all the facts and he took charge, and decided to wait and try again. I then spoke to an off duty policewoman who had kindly offered her assistance, and she pursuaded the old lady to leave the train.

The train departed twenty minutes late and when I reported the delay and the reason to Line Control, I had to smile at the thought of the old lady hitting the policeman, but yet another problem had been solved.

Redundancy was a word to fear on the railway, and rumours had been going about that Rotherham Control Office and Sheffield Control Office at Sheffield (Victoria) Station were to join up as one at Sheaf House, just outside Sheffield (Midland) Station. It was thought that the Section Controllers would be all right with just the circuits being moved but, except for a few senior assistants, the rest would go.

Rumour turned to fact, and on 7th September 1966 my world was in ruins for I received, along with several of my workmates, notice of redundancy. It coldly read 'I regret to inform you that in connection with the new staffing arrangements in the new Sheffield Control Office you have not been accommodated in a position and you will therefore become redundant in the post you occupy at the present from 12/9/66, and it is necessary to give you five months notice expiring on 11/2/67'. The letter went on to say that I would be temporarily employed in the new Control Office until I left the service in February. It took a long time for the letter to register, but I had to face the fact that I was going to be out of a job.

I felt rather sad and bitter, wistfully thinking that if I had stopped in my first signal box at Kilnhurst I would still have a job. Instead I had gone for promotion and, by leaving the signalling grade because of the threat of redundancy, I was now working out my time.

The new Control Office was then opened, covering a large area of railway including my old line from Mexborough to Rotherham, so I was reunited with some old signalling mates, even if it was to be only for a short time. I was placed, along with several others, as a spare duty man to cover any Assistant Controller's position on any shift, in case of illness or holidays. I was working on a day to day basis, and one typical working week read; Monday 9 a.m. spare, Tuesday 6 a.m. General Assistant, Wednesday and Thursday 2 p.m. Duty Chief Controller Assistant, Friday 6 a.m. spare, Saturday, rest day. I had to check the notice-board daily for alterations, and with no overtime, no rest day working, no weekend working and not even any night duty, I was only on basic wages.

A Controller has to know his section, so occasionally he is sent out of the office to look over his section, meet the people with whom he is in daily contact, and see for himself the outside problems. A kind Controller, who had been my chief at the old Rotherham office, saw I was getting very disillusioned and, as he had plenty of spare men, sent me out for a week to look over the Sheffield Area with which I was not familiar. I was delighted as I had been given a whole week just to travel, and the best

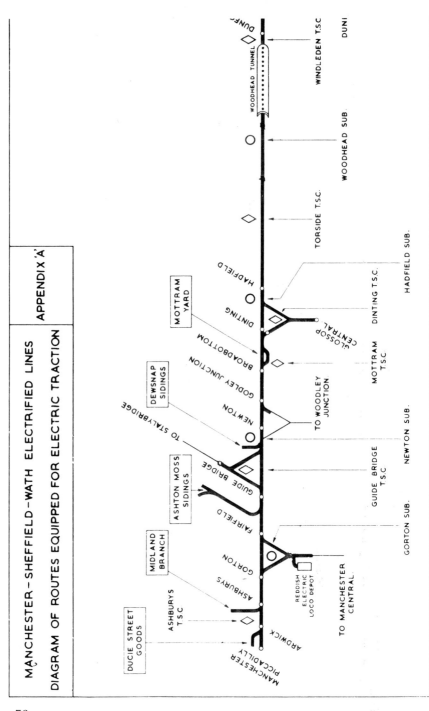

## MANCHESTER–SHEFFIELD–WATH ELECTRIFIED LINES

### APPENDIX 'A'

## DIAGRAM OF ROUTES EQUIPPED FOR ELECTRIC TRACTION

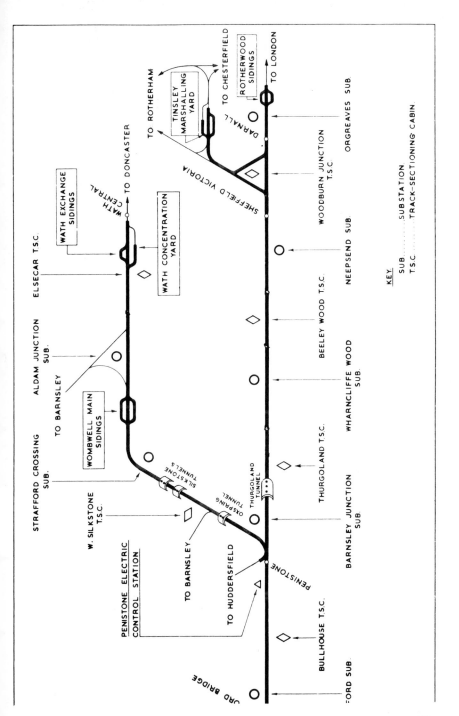

77

news was that I could have an engine pass meaning I could travel, with the drivers' permission, on any train to see the branch lines, goods yards and junctions, that before had just been names on a timetable. To a railwayman who was still very keen at heart, it was a holiday with pay.

I had to report to Control daily to see if I was required for duty but on this Monday morning, as I collected the engine pass, my day was already planned out. However, it turned out better than was planned.

I walked across the famous steel city to Sheffield (Victoria) Station, to have a look at the Manchester to Sheffield electrified lines. I had a copy of the working instructions for this line, with its own 122 rules, but I had only learnt one small section off by heart. I knew the steel structures to carry the wires were placed 210 ft. apart and that the normal height of the wires was 16 ft. above high rail level, increased to 18 ft. at public road level crossings.

The engine pass covered passenger trains so I had decided to travel up to Penistone Station so, after showing the driver my pass and obtaining his permission to travel with him, I climbed aboard the engine.

On the electric engine on this service the driver did not have a mate, so I sat in the other seat to wait for the journey to start. The passenger trains ran about every hour, on an hour long journey over some beautiful countryside.

At 9.45 a.m. we started with a light load of five coaches, and gained speed as we climbed up to Wadsley Bridge Station then, while passing Deepcar and then Barnsley Junction, I told the driver why I was on this train and found that, like most drivers, he was a keen railwayman and pleased to pass on his knowledge.

He pointed sidings out to me and told me all about the line, but we were too soon approaching Penistone Station where I would have to leave the train and, as I would be out of the Sheffield Area, my pass would not be valid. I thanked the driver for his help and wished him a safe journey to Manchester but then, to my surprise, he told me that although he could not accept any responsibility for me on the engine I could, if I wanted to, go all the way to Manchester then back to Sheffield with him at my own risk, as he would be glad of some company.

I took the chance of a lifetime knowing that if anything went wrong I would be in trouble, but considered it worth the gamble as I was already almost out of a job on the railway.

We departed from Penistone Station and were soon passing some very beautiful scenery, with moors reaching out on both sides of the track, for the Peak District is very wild but exciting in a bleak sort of way. Then, after passing Dunford Bridge, we entered the famous Woodhead Tunnel.

I thought the tunnel was a level road and was surprised to find a falling gradient, but now I could see the faint glimmer of daylight at the end of the tunnel getting larger until, with a rush, we were out of the darkness into the very bright light of the open air and the breathtaking stretch of line. The Bleaklow Moors were on our left and, on the right-hand side, first Woodhead Reservoir then Torside Rhodeswood and Vale-house reservoirs, glittering in the morning sunshine.

It must have been a hard railway to work on in the days of steam when, in the middle of winter, after nearly choking in the tunnel, the enginemen were exposed to the harsh bleakness and cold of the moors but here, in the warm cab, I felt on top of world.

We passed Dinting, now travelling on the London Midland Region, and then Mottram Yard, a place my father often talked about as the coldest yard that Mexborough men ever worked to. Next was Godley Junction and, with the traffic and track becoming more congested, I sat quiet letting the driver concentrate on his difficult task of getting his train past Guide Bridge and into his destination of Manchester (Piccadilly) Station.

We had a break in Manchester and then I had a similar return journey to Sheffield (Victoria), where again I thanked the driver. I wondered if the passengers we had safely carried realized the years of training and dedication behind such men, who daily carried out their tasks in all weathers so they could travel and arrive on time in safety.

The rest of the week passed all too quickly, but I saw plenty of the area.

In January 1967, I was temporarily transferred to Tinsley Yard to work in the Main Yard Control Tower on a charting scheme.

I handed in my Control telephone headset and left the office, wondering if I would ever return. With no choice this time, I set off again to yet another adventure.

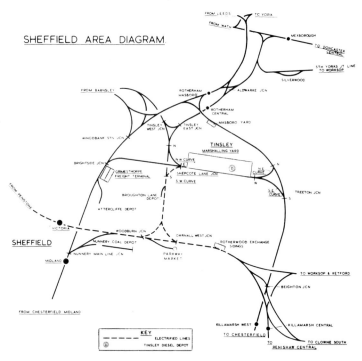

SHEFFIELD AREA DIAGRAM.

```
CONSISTS 8 P45 0731  WATH IMMINGHAM  2/6/67
D1800
30  17049   CW2 1/6 H MANVERS IMM   S/S CHELWOOD
30  98146   +
30  209335  +
30  20906B  +
30  90009   +  + + WENTWORTH +   S/S PULLBORO
30  142474  +
30  162197  +
30  150437  +
30  211004  +
30  571186  +
31  557024  +  30/5    +    + S/S CORCHESTER
31  587439  +
31  558344  +
31  589480  +
31  558590  +
30  103941  +  1/6    +    + S/S PULLBORO
30  242798  +
30  235948  +
30  153703  +
30  81860   +
30  173939  +
30  185453  +
30  145956  +
30  619862  +
30  214293  +
30  137074  +
30  41809   +
30  74217   +
30  575528  +
30  212003  +
30  255603  +
30  568828  +
30  95735   +
30  231101  +
FBV 954484
34=68
TRAIN DEP 0820
```

Sample telex as despatched by the Author whilst at Wath Yard.

80

# Chapter Ten
# Tinsley Yard

Tinsley Yard is situated between Rotherham and Sheffield and is principally a terminal yard for the Sheffield Area, being designed for two-way working.

The yard was an £11 million scheme, and the first in the world to be equipped with the Dowty System of Automatic Wagon Control. In the past, the Sheffield Area had dozens of small sidings and yards, mainly for the steel traffic, the trouble being that some sidings were part of the Great Central Railway and others the Midland Railway. Thus it was decided to centralize everything into one large yard and join both railways together, with traffic running to and from all directions, and the yard was opened in October 1964.

It has four distinct operating areas; Reception Sidings, Main Yard Sorting Sidings, Secondary Sorting Sidings and Express Freight & Departure Sidings. Within the yard boundaries are a diesel locomotive maintenance depot and a servicing depot.

The reception sidings have eleven reception lines, each with capacities of between 63 to 74 wagons, a hump engine return line and an engine line. The lines Nos. 6 to 11 are electrified, as an extension to the Manchester, Sheffield and Wath electrification system.

Trains from the north-west curve (Tinsley East) and the south-east curve (Broughton Lane) run via North West Arrival and North Hump Approach into sidings Nos. 1 to 8. Trains from the north-east curve and south-east curve ran direct into all eleven sidings.

The Main Yard Sorting Sidings had 53 sidings, the capacity of these varying from 53 to 80 wagons. Departures are normally westward bound, and those from sidings Nos. 16 to 48 proceed via the West Departure line. Eastbound services from sidings Nos. 1 to 19 are drawn back into the Express Freight Sidings, before departing by a connection at the western end of the main yard.

All the sidings up to No. 48 have a siding allocation for the following destinations; No. 2 Toton (fitted), No. 10 Washwood Heath (fitted), No. 13 Healey Mills (unfitted), No. 16 Feed Road, No. 20 Hull, No. 21 York, No. 24 Leicester and London and No. 36 South Wales. These are a few examples, showing that trains from Tinsley Yard ran to destinations all over the country.

The Secondary Sidings were Nos. 60 to 84 each holding 31 wagons, and traffic is routed here direct from the Main Yard via the Dowty Mechanical Feed Road. Most of the destinations for the wagons were only local to Wath, Rotherham and Sheffield.

The express freight sidings were designed to accommodate through express freight trains required to detach and or attach merchandise traffic, and there were only five sidings in that group.

There are two Control Towers. The Main Yard Control Tower, at the entrance to the Main Yard Sorting Sidings, is a four storey building and the room on the top floor, the operating room where I was working, gave a bird's-eye view of the yard. The other Control Tower is at the Secondary Sidings.

The diesel locomotive servicing shed is situated near the hump and comprises a four berth through shed with facilities for refuelling, lubricating and examining locomotives together with ancilliary workshops, stores and office accommodation. A locomotive washing plant is provided here, and it is also the home of the breakdown crane. The diesel maintenance depot or 'top shed' is double-ended, with twelve berths, a workshop and stores.

This was my first visit to Tinsley Yard, and the Inspector explained how it all worked. When a train arrives on the reception line the 'cutter' (shunter) examines the wagons and records the details in code on a cut card. The wagons are then uncoupled. The cut card shows the intended sorting siding, the number of wagons in each cut and any special information. With a high degree of automation in the operation of the humping process, accurate details must be made, and these details are transmitted to the Control Tower.

The receiving instrument in the Control Tower prints out the information and, at the same time, produces a punched tape for feeding into the point setting control machine when the train is about to be hump-shunted. The machine will automatically set the points for each cut in both the Main and Secondary sidings.

The humping units were two 350 hp diesel locomotives which were fitted with cab signalling, precision speedometers and 2 two-way radio telephones. They push the wagons over the hump, and then a bank of booster retarder units accelerate the cuts of wagons up to 7/8 m.p.h., and maintains them at that speed clear of the next points. Once clear of the points further banks of retarder units reduce the speed of the wagons from 5 m.p.h. to 2 m.p.h., until a safe buffing speed is reached.

I found the Dowtry System of Automatic Wagon Control very interesting with wagons on the move all the time, just missing one another as they clattered along towards the sidings without a shunter in sight. It was a far cry from my shunting days.

My charting job was mostly telephone work involving details of local trip trains working into Tinsley, so I could pass on the advance information to the Inspectors. I received a letter on 20th February to say my services will continue to be utilized until further notice, so this job had been a temporary reprieve.

Early one morning, just before the end of the night shift, the Control rang the Tower Inspector to ascertain the whereabouts of a freight train as the engine was required at Sheffield (Midland) Station to work a slow passenger train to Leeds, the booked engine having failed.

As the call was nothing to do with my duties, I did not pay much attention to it until I saw the engine go past, a rare sight, an LMS Black Five, No. 44852. All the passenger trains on that route were now diagrammed as diesel-hauled but the only engine now available of the right class was this steam engine. It had looked out of place in a modern railway yard, but now it had to be used.

I quickly realized that this would be the last steam-hauled booked passenger working, so when my relief arrived I jumped into the car to rush home for my cine camera to record on film a little piece of local railway history; the last steam-hauled passenger train to stop at Swinton (Midland) Station. I arrived in time to take my film and then returned home to go to bed, only to realize that I had made a mistake by not catching the train with more film, but now, of course, it was too late.

In April 1967 I was still at Tinsley Yard, but a vacancy arose for a Class 3 clerk as a telex operator in connection with advance traffic information at Wath Yard, very close to home. It was a lower grade but regular job so I applied, got the job, beat the redundancy notice and yet again moved to another branch of railway operation.

I had to pass a telex training course in London but then I returned to my old line, the Great Central Railway at Wath Yard, and found life again different, a lot slower than signalling on the GNR, and more relaxed than life in the Control Office.

I sat in my small office while the trains passed by only a few feet away, and felt again that I was back working on a living railway with all the atmosphere and noise of wagons bumping and engines moving, and, with the presence of local men who I had known for years, I was feeling very much at home once again.

The object of advance traffic information was to send freight train details in advance, and this was how it worked. A shunter would walk round a train with a miniature tape recorder and record the details of each wagon. The tape would then be returned to my office where I put on an earset and type out the message on to a punched tape. This tape was then transmitted by telex, with the teleprinter network giving out a printed copy at both the sending and receiving stations.

By dialling a telex number, the train details were sent to other yards with copies going to the Divisional Manager, the information giving the other yards all the train details even before the train had left Wath Yard. This was used to help the pre-planning of yard workings. The wagon details were recorded in code in the following order; type of wagon, wagon number, route code, label date, wagon weight, special traffic notes, sending station, destination station and consignee. The wagon code was simple in that a 16 ton mineral wagon was No. 30 and a bogie bolster A was No. 48, and all types of wagons were coded in this manner. Thus a print-out for each wagon would read so; 30 17049 CW2 1/6 H MANVERS IMMINGHAM S/S CHELWOOD. The train details were also sent.

Inward calls were received in the same manner and prefixed with the sending code sign for example, Rail Immingham. My code was Rail Wath, and as the machine was never switched off you could leave it for half an hour and, on returning, find a full consist there waiting, fully typed out, prior to being passed to the Area Yard Manager.

Speed of operation was slow at first but, as the weeks passed, with practice, the typing became quicker. Only a few yards were coupled to the telex as it was a new idea to British Rail so only a small amount of messages were sent meaning that, apart from some clerical work, the job was easy. This was just as well, because with only three operators to cover around the clock, if anyone was off work, either sick or on holiday, the others had to cover and, as we were all working on rest days, a lot of overtime was done. The normal rate of pay was about £20 per week, but most weeks we all earned nearly twice that amount.

After a year at Wath, I was bored with the lack of interest and the very long hours so, when a vacancy for a list clerk at Rotherham came on the list, I decided to try for promotion, succeeded, and moved up to clerk (Class 2).

# Chapter Eleven
# List Clerks Duties

I was introduced to my new mate, Trainsman Inspector Jimmy Bird, an ex-LMS engine driver, and straight away we got on very well together while covering all aspects of the job. Jim knew all about enginemen, engines, diagrams and LMS railway routes while I, for my part, knew about signalling, Control, routes on the other railway, and the clerical work.

It is a well-known fact that drivers and guards do not always see eye to eye with signalman and Control but here I was, having worked both jobs, among the train crews and finding them to be good railwaymen.

An engine driver's work is highly-skilled, complicated and complex, requiring a very high standard of ability. Yet here I was with only a little knowledge, most of that freely given by the train crews at Wath Yard after they knew I was entering their world, in addition to what my father had taught me at home together with what I had read, to solve the intricate working of diagrams, single manning, bonus sheets, passed fireman driving and clerical work at a trainsmen relief depot. Despite this I was not worried because I had an experienced man in charge of the depot sat at the next desk who, in the great railway tradition, was only too pleased to help with his vast knowledge and experience.

As a rest day relief man I did not start to compile the roster duties but only to alter them, owing to train crews' sickness or leave, and the Trainsman Inspector assisted me with this task and, as it was only a small depot, there were not many problems.

Special train circulars and notices were received at the office and, apart from making sure all the train crews were issued with them, they were also sent to the signal boxes, yard foreman, station foreman, stationmaster's office and the signal & telegraph staff. The notices were mainly details for alterations in Sunday work, so it was important that they were all issued early.

A list clerk had to sign all train crews on and off duty, and with the payment of wages outside office hours and a switchboard to operate, it was a busy but interesting job of work.

As a rest day relief I did not work nights or weekends, so a week was split up into day and afternoon shifts except on Thursdays, when I worked from 9 a.m. to 5 p.m. in the wages office handing out the money.

One day I had to find a train crew to travel to an out of the way place, miles away from a passenger station, but on the normal freight route, so I had to find a bus so the men could travel out on it. The men were required on a Tuesday, but the bus only ran on Mondays or Wednesdays, so when I asked Jim if the train could be altered either a day forward or backwards he burst out laughing and told me to book the men on duty in good time so that the Trainsmen Inspector on duty that day could arrange for the crew to travel on a passing freight train. It took a long time for me to live that down, due to lack of experience.

On quiet moments, such as 9 p.m. on a Saturday winter evening, I used to enjoy listening to the train crews talking about routes and past experiences, particularly the older drivers with their stories of steam, and from them I learnt about routes, loads, and good and bad trips.

One story which I found very funny concerned something that happened to my mate. He was driving a steam engine over the Hope Valley line, between Sheffield and Manchester, a very bleak line through the Derbyshire hills, and during one very bad winter the snow was falling fast so, after leaving his train in Hope Sidings, he decided to turn the engine to face the right way for the weather for the journey back home to the Chesterfield area.

He stopped the engine short of the turntable to check if the table was clear of snow and in working order, and then climbed off the engine. As he is only small he disappeared into a large snow drift and had to be dragged out, wet and cold, by the fireman and guard.

Rumours were circulating about more railway closures, so when a vacancy came up for a regular list clerk of the same class as at Tinsley Yard I applied, deciding that it would be a safer depot than Rotherham and I would be making the rosters up from scratch instead of just daily alterations. I was accepted and moved back to Tinsley in September 1969, after spending a happy year at Rotherham (Masborough) in which I learnt my trade as a list clerk. I arrived for my second spell at Tinsley Yard, near Sheffield, at a salary of £930 per annum but this time I was in the main administration building in the office block.

All train crews are placed in links; that is a set of diagram workings of twelve sets of men in a link, working a twelve week cycle. The links are governed by seniority, with the long service men in the top links working express passenger and express freight trains and the less senior men working freight and local trip trains, and shunting pilots. A driver with years of experience would have worked his way through all the links, while a secondman would also have worked through the links then, after becoming a driver, he started in the bottom link.

There were seventeen links for the locomotive men at Tinsley Yard and most of the diagrams were, of course, for freight trains. A driver did not always sign on duty at the same time every day, nor did he work the same train every day, this being due to working different diagrams, so in the same week he could work trains to several destinations.

Each set of locomotive men worked five days a week with a rest day off, this rest day falling on a Saturday in week one, Wednesday in week three and Tuesday in week four so, in a twelve week cycle, all days were covered, giving two long weekend breaks when rest day Saturday was followed by rest day Monday. Some examples of the workings from the top link No. 1 at Tinsley Yard are shown in the Table on page 87.

As seen from the diagrams, in week No. 10 the time on duty moved from 23.59 Monday to 18.15 spare on Friday, or the time on duty moved either up or down as illustrated in week No. 5. The roster work was started on the Monday night shift, to be ready for pinning on the noticeboard for Thursday morning along with the alterations to the next week's work. It took three nights of hard work and this is how we did it, taking link No. 1 as an example.

| | Monday | Tuesday | Wednesday | Thursday | Friday | Saturday |
|---|---|---|---|---|---|---|
| WEEK NO. 1 | | | | | | |
| TIME ON DUTY | 0100 | 0128 | 0128 | 0128 | 0128 | REST DAY |
| TRAIN DEST. | - | YORK | YORK | YORK | YORK | - |
| DIA. NO. | - | 531 | 531 | 531 | 531 | - |
| WEEK NO. 5 | | | | | | |
| TIME ON DUTY | 0533 | 0258 | 0258 | 0258 | REST DAY | 0625 |
| TRAIN DEST. | H MILLS | LINCOLN | LINCOLN | LINCOLN | - | DERBY |
| DIA. NO. | 426 | 435 | 435 | 435 | - | 524 |
| WEEK NO. 6 | | | | | | |
| TIME ON DUTY | 1535 | same | same | same | same | REST DAY |
| TRAIN DEST. | BRANSTON | same | same | same | same | - |
| DIA. NO. | 412 | 412 | 412 | 412 | 412 | - |
| WEEK NO. 10 | | | | | | |
| TIME ON DUTY | 2359 | 2020 | 1903 | 1815 | 1815 | REST DAY |
| TRAIN DEST. | SPARE | YORK | H MILLS | SPARE | SPARE | REST DAY |

LINK NUMBER ONE TINSLEY YARD

The links were printed on several boards so I placed the names of the following week's men at the side of the diagrams, and any man that would be missing was crossed off. Sick or injured, annual leave, compensatory leave, working as Supervisor, road learning, eyesight or medical examinations, technical examinations or railway competitions all took men off booked diagrams, and meant they had to be replaced. I used a large sheet of paper to record the vacant diagrams so by the time link No. 17 was reached I had a full list of jobs to cover. Most links had a driver with a booked spare week so these men were listed on to another sheet, and placed into vacant diagrams.

This was the hard part for several reasons. A spare man could only be moved two hours either side of his booked time on duty, so if he was 06.00 spare I could only move him between 04.00 and 08.00. If this time factor was not enough, the other big problem was route knowledge, which is explained later.

This week the diagrams to cover were at 01.28 and 15.35 time on duty in link No. 1, and the spare man was 23.59. I could only move him to 21.59, the other way meaning another days working, so he was out and still left spare for now. I now moved to link No. 2 which had a spare at 03.13 on duty, so he covered the 01.28 diagram in link No. 1. My link No. 1 driver was still unplaced, with nothing vacant in his time in link No. 2, so he moved to link No. 3 to cover the 22.29 diagram No. 404, destination York. He worked to York in his own link, so route knowledge was no problem.

Every driver, passed fireman and guard has a route knowledge card, and at Tinsley Yard it covered over 200 routes. Some destinations were routed different ways with Scarborough having five routes and Blackpool having nine and, because of the maize of local lines even a nearby siding could be reached several ways.

Tinsley men worked to Morecambe, Llandudno, London, Banbury, New England and also to depots near to home base, but if a driver no longer felt competent to work safely over a route, he would cancel that route off his card and sign it, so a list clerk would check the card for any alterations.

| TURN NO. | Arrive | THAIN WORKING | Depart | W.T.T. No. | ACT AS SECOND MAN To Dvr. | Stan. Term. Bonus Mins. | Non Running Time | BASE ALLOW'CES Term. Minutes Mins. |
|---|---|---|---|---|---|---|---|---|
| 22b SX | | On Duty 11 40 MSX. Tinsley MY | 12 35 | 8N86 | | | | |
| | 14 50 | York Yd. No. | 14 55 | LE | | | | |
| | 14 01 | York Depot | 15 17 | LE | | | | |
| | 15 25 | York S.N.S. | 15 42 | 8J84 | | | | |
| | 17 48 | Tinsley RL | 17 54 | LE | | | | |
| | 18 03 | Tinsley Depot Off Duty 19 40 | | 8 00 | | | | |
| SO | | On Duty 11 40 SO Tinsley MY | 12 35 | 8N86 | | | | |
| | 14 52 | York Yd. No. Relieved | | | | | | |
| | | York Depot | 15 54 | LE | TIN.461 | | | |
| | 16 00 | York Yard No. | 16 10 | 8M14 | | | | |
| | 18 03 | Masborough Relieved by Passr. by 18 20 service car to Tinsley Off duty 19 40 | | 8 00 | | | | |
| 227 SX | 17 33 | On Duty 17 08 SX. Tinsley MYE | 17 35 | 9J75 | | | | |
| | 18 21 | Barrow Hill | 18 32 | 0M39 | TIN.452 | | | |
| | 18 46 | Seymour Jcn. | 19 50 | 9M39 | | | | |
| | 20 29 | Rotherwood | 21 17 | 0J68 | TIN.452 | | | |
| | 21 38 | Treeton South | 22 05 | 9J68 | | | | |
| | 22 30 | Barrow Hill | 23 05 | 9J52 | | | | |
| | 23 43 | Tinsley RL | 23 49 | LE | TIN.452 | | | |
| | 23 55 | Tinsley Depot Off duty 01 08 Hours   8 00 | | | | | | |
| 228 SO | | On Duty 12 26 SO Tinsley Depot | 12 51 | LE | TIN.422 | | | |
| | 13 17 | Rotherwood | 13 30 | 7E30 | | | | |
| | 14 54 | Boultham Jcn. Relieved by WM.103 Passenger by 15 50 Lincoln to Worksop. Worksop D.S.P. | 17 48 | LE | TIN.422 | | | |
| | 17 51 | Worksop D.S. | 18 00 | 9J28 | | | | |
| | 19 12 | Tinsley R.L. | 19 18 | LE | TIN.422 | | | |
| | 19 27 | Tinsley Depot Off Duty 20 26 Hours   8.00. | | | | | | |

Freight guards diagram for Tinsley Depot.

B.R. 32707/6
B.R. 32707/5

# BRITISH RAILWAYS    ROUTE KNOWLEDGE CARD

Depot: TINSLEY    Name .................................................    No........................

(in Block Letters)

Grade.........................................

| Section of Line | Certification | | Cancellation | |
|---|---|---|---|---|
| | Initials | Date | Initials | Date |
| Aldwarke via Brightside Jnc. | | | | |
| Aldwarke via Tinsley East | | | | |
| Aldwarke via Treeton Jnc. | | | | |
| Aintree Loco. | | | | |
| Ancoats | | | | |
| Ardwick | | | | |
| Arpley via Skelton Jnc | | | | |
| Ashburys | | | | |
| Ashton Jnc | | | | |
| Attercliffe Yard | | | | |
| Barnetby via Retford | | | | |
| Banbury via Clowne | | | | |
| Barnsley via Chapeltown | | | | |
| Barnsley Jnc. via Barnsley | | | | |
| Barnsley Jnc. via Deepcar | | | | |
| Barnsley Jnc via Mexborough | | | | |
| Bedford | | | | |
| Beighton Jnc. via Darnall | | | | |
| Beighton Jnc. via Treeton | | | | |
| Beighton Engrs. Depot | | | | |
| Barrow Hill | | | | |
| Bernard Road | | | | |
| Belle Vue | | | | |
| Birmingham Lawley Street via Kingsbury East Line | | | | |
| Birmingham Lawley Street via Kingsbury and Whitacre | | | | |
| Birmingham New Street | | | | |
| Boston via Lincoln | | | | |
| Boultham Jnc | | | | |
| Bourneville | | | | |
| Brent Sidings | | | | |
| Brookhouse | | | | |
| Burnley | | | | |
| Burton via Ambergate and Derby | | | | |
| Burton via Trowell and Castle Donnington | | | | |
| Buxton via Ambergate | | | | |
| Buxton via Edale and Peak Forest Jnc. | | | | |
| Carnforth | | | | |
| Chaddlesden Sidings | | | | |

British Railways Route knowledge card for Tinsley Depot.

The route knowledge was abundant in the higher links, due to the drivers' experience, but lower down it was sometimes a problem. This was because Tinsley was a new depot and men from the old LMS sheds of Canklow or Grimethorpe knew the LMS routes and not the old LNER routes, and men from Darnall Shed knew the LNER routes and not the LMS, but as men had road learning, it was always getting easier.

The moving of spare men went on right through all the links until all the diagrams were covered, and after the drivers' diagrams were all filled, the same had to apply with the secondmen, but this was a lot easier with no route knowledge and single-manned turns. The guards' diagrams were then covered by the same method.

When the full weeks working had all been done, it often had to be altered again if a driver went off sick, so it was a continuous task. A daily sheet alteration was made out to cover men with a few or just one day off, and again it was done in the same manner. Most links had men with one or two days spare a week (see week No. 10, Thursday and Friday) so again the higher link men were used first, but there were pitfalls.

If a driver was rest day, Wednesday, he could not start work before 04.00 Thursday, so if he was 05.00 spare, the time limit was only from 04.00 to 07.00. Therefore I had to check back or forward a day because in link No. 3 (week No. 7) the driver was 04.00 spare and the day after he was on duty at 01.03, so if he was moved to 06.00 he would not finish his eight hours until 14.00. Also, because he had to have twelve hours off duty between shifts, he could not start again until 02.00, nearly an hour late for his booked turn of duty.

When a driver could not be found to cover a diagram, I had to upgrade a passed secondman to a driver. Again it had to be within the two hours limit, with route knowledge and seniority again being the key. This meant that the secondman's job had to be covered, but this was easy as I could upgrade a passed cleaner (again senior men first).

Alterations were being made all the time to the daily lists, because if all the train crews were booked work then the Freight Movements Office at York would put on a special train, usually at short notice.

A circular received on a Wednesday would require a train crew for the following Friday to work the (8Z49) 07.00 Burton upon Trent to York train. Tinsley men and guard would work the train, which would run light engine from Tinsley at 05.00, to work back to Rotherham (Masborough) ready for the relief crew. I had to book the men on duty with enough time to prepare the engine and read notices, so Friday's list had to be altered again. When there was a spate of special trains to cover, or a 'flu epidemic, it provided a lot of work for a list clerk.

Sunday working was another problem because of the many ballast trains to man for engineering work, and an up to date record was kept of the number of Sundays a man had worked, so that everyone had a fair share of the overtime working. The record also showed what shift was last worked, to avoid a man working his last three Sundays all at 4 a.m. in the morning or 9 p.m. at night.

A train crew on long weekend (i.e. rest day Saturday and Monday) would not be considered unless they so requested and, with a Sunday roster, Monday's duties had to be carefully watched, to avoid a driver being late for his booked diagram work. Bank holiday workings were also arranged the same as Sundays.

Another problem with so many alterations to the daily list was men going home and their next turn of duty being altered in their absence, although it was mainly passed secondmen promoted to a driving turn that were affected. Tinsley has no passenger station, so a small railway bus ran between the yard and Sheffield (Midland) and Rotherham stations, for the purpose of ferrying train crews. When it was not required for that task, the driver's mate would call at a man's home and leave a card with the details of his next turn of duty upon it, rather like the old 'caller up'.

When a man was booked to work the night shift, he received more money, so if I took him off his booked diagram to go road learning in the daytime, his wages were either his own hours worked, or the same as the man who worked his diagram at night, whichever was the greater. This meant that he did not, in fact, lose any overtime payments.

With any large train crew depot there were a few problems with the diagram workings; mainly passed secondmen claiming driving turns. In any dispute the local LDC men would call into the office and between us, we would solve any train crew problems.

Railway work goes on around the clock, and a list clerk was kept busy on all shifts. He had to make sure that the other men knew what he had already done and why, so they in turn could alter his daily sheets or take over the rosters where he had left off.

A list clerk works days and weeks in advance, but the real problem of hour by hour working is the Trainmen Inspector's headache. Engine failure, derailment, fog, falling snow, or the many other items that would alter and slow down normal depot working were dealt with on the spot.

A set of train crews could sign on duty as a booked diagram, only to find out that the train was running five hours late, so they would not have time to work the train forward to its destination. So another duty had to be found for them, then a new crew, later on duty, were utilized to work the late train.

If traffic to one destination was light, then the AYM and Control could cancel the diagram, the train being sent forward as a special working to another destination with the same crew, if they all had the route knowledge. If not, another crew or a 'foreign' crew would be used. Sometimes, I have spent up to half a day working to cover a diagram two days in advance, only to find on the day that the diagram is cancelled at short notice.

My job was still busy but I noticed, over a period of time, a sharp decrease in the movement of rail traffic due to the nearby M1 motorway gaining all the traffic.

Freight train crews who, for years, had to endure very long hours were now going home after less than eight hours on duty, and sometimes after not even working a train. An increasing number of trains were being cancelled because of the lack of goods to carry. Crews were riding home instead of back-working and in the train crews' mess room, there were more crews than there were trains to work. Large sidings, locomotive depots and signal boxes were all closing, and the chance for promotion had almost gone with the few vacancies all being taken, rightly so, by the redundant men. Where could I move now? What did the future hold for me on British Rail? If train crews were not required then neither were list clerks, and I was again the junior man.

# Chapter Twelve
# Reflections

I handed in my notice of resignation and left the service of British Rail in October 1970. For the first few weeks I could not settle but this soon passed, as I could now enjoy a nine to five working day with no more starting at 5 a.m. in the morning or working Sunday nights.

After fourteen years spent on the railway, what had I achieved? In a short career I had occupied positions with plenty of interest, and had met and worked with plenty of good railwaymen. The best times are hard to define, but two stand out above the others. The first was my years as a lad in Mexborough No. 3 box, with all the happy hours spent on the circuit telephone. The second was the Saturday shifts in the summer season as a signalman at Doncaster South, with all the passenger trains running in and out of the station or on the main line. It was very hectic work but very rewarding, especially when all the trains ran into the right platforms at the right time without delay. To all the many railwaymen who helped me over the years, I thank you all.

I find it sad to see so many signal boxes not only closed but pulled down, with the tracks removed and very few trains now passing. Mexborough Station is all that is left of a very busy railway depot, as the engine sheds are now grass and the shunting yards are just a memory. Also, in place of the once busy signal boxes, there are now just a few colour light signals, worked from a box miles away in Sheffield. The boxes at Retford and Doncaster are now worked by one power box, as the line between Sheffield (Victoria) and Manchester is now closed to all services. Lastly, Rotherham train crew depot is no longer functioning but Tinsley Yard is still open, albeit on a smaller scale.

Railways have changed but I still enjoy a ride on the Doncaster to King's Cross main line, by courtesy of a 125 m.p.h. HST that does the 156 miles in 99 minutes or less. This is compared with the 136 minutes that a 'Deltic' required when I was a signalman or, the 163 minutes that a steam engine took when I was a lad. I wonder what times *Mallard* on the 'Flying Scotsman' could do now, with the faster track and the colour light signalling; but that we will never know.

The railway is now a hobby, and plenty of preservation societies' books keep my interest, while in my loft I am building a model railway, modelled on the last days of steam. Photographs are pinned to the walls and there is an old rule book on the shelf but, taking pride over everything else, is a full size copy of a signal box diagram of my second box, Thrybergh Junction. On a quiet winter's night, as I look at the diagram and see a model freight train slowly moving past, I can almost hear again the bells ringing, the levers moving, and the telephone circuit going.

*Above:* Mexborough Station.

*Below:* The 'up' Bournemouth to York express speeds past Mexborough No. 3 box behind Thompson B1 No. 61071.

*Above:* An 'up' passenger train from Sheffield (Victoria) to Doncaster stands at Kilnhurst in 1961.

*Below:* Doncaster South power box.                    *OPC/British Rail*